Our

Warfare

Our

Warfare

T. Austin-Sparks

LIFE SENTENCE Publishing, LLC

RELIGION / Christianity / General

ISBN 13: 978-0-9832016-2-5

Available from the Publishers at:

(at the price of your choice)
www.lifesentencepublishing.com
715.223.3013

Also available from:
Amazon.com
Barnesandnoble.com
And more...

Printed in the United States of America

Contents

Publisher's Note

Jeremiah M. Zeiset
LIFE SENTENCE Publishing, LLC
Wisconsin, US, 2011

Preface

The following chapters were given as messages at a conference in Honor Oak, London. Whilst a considerable background of spiritual experience in the service of God lies behind them, the form in which the messages were given was prompted by a reading of that great volume by Field Marshal Sir William Slim—*Defeat into Victory*. Every chapter really needs a book to itself, as there is far more unwritten than is contained in this small book.

At the present time, as the consummation of the age draws nearer and the final settlement is in view, the battle which divides the universe into only two contending kingdoms is raging fiercely and relentlessly. It is therefore necessary that everything possible be done to inform, instruct, counsel, warn, encourage, and support those who are involved and affected. We appeal to all who read these pages, not to approach their message in any attitude of mere interest or theory, but to study them as though they themselves were directly involved in the tremendous issues at stake.

To leaders, and others in responsibility, we especially appeal, that they would consider what is here in the light of their own present experience of a "great warfare" (Dan. 10:1). If leaders would but get together to review this whole matter of the spiritual conflict, more might be accomplished in the direction of turning Defeat into Victory.

Should Field Marshal Slim's eye ever catch sight of this volume, I hope that—rather than resenting it—he will be glad that his great reversal in the earthly realm may serve, even in a small way, to affect the so-much-greater realm of the eternal and heavenly.

T. AUSTIN SPARKS

FOREST HILL,

LONDON,

1960.

Supreme Command

*"For though we walk in the flesh, we do not war according to the
flesh (for the weapons of OUR WARFARE are not of the flesh, but
mighty before God to the casting down of strong holds)"
(2 Corinthians 10:3–4).*

Although the Bible contains so much about the warfare of
God's people, and although we as His people may have had
much teaching on the subject, it would probably be true to
say that we have largely failed to apply the instruction we
have received—to situations, to circumstances, to
happenings; and that this accounts for many of our troubles,
individually and collectively. While there is much for which

the enemy is not to be blamed as the first cause, but which is due rather to our own foolishness or unguardedness—our own faults—yet there is still very much more that is attributable to his interest, to his interference, and to his action. Our need today is not so much to be informed as to the reality of spiritual conflict—we know that to be a fact!— as to be more alive to the extra factor lying behind situations, the situations with which we are trying, with so little success, to cope. We try to cope with things, as though they were everything, and so often we miss their real underlying significance.

What we need, therefore, is understanding and wisdom — for wisdom means the ability to apply knowledge—wisdom as to this whole spiritual campaign, our warfare and its principles. But let me say at once: we are not embarking upon a study of Satan, or demons, or demonology! It is a very favorite trap of the enemy to get people occupied and obsessed with himself, and, by the help of God, we are not going to fall into that. Our object is to study spiritual warfare itself, as viewed mainly from the Lord's side.

Let me here put in a brief word as to the origin, or occasion, of the messages here presented. Not having a great deal of time for general reading, I make it a matter of prayer that all my serious reading may be spiritually profitable and of value—whether it be reading a spiritual book or not. Just before leaving on a recent voyage to the United States, I was exercised in this manner, when a book came to my notice, and an extract from it arrested me. It was the record of the great South East Asia campaign in the second World War, and was entitled *Defeat into Victory*. It is a heavy volume of 550 closely printed pages, with an added 23 for index. But having been arrested by this extract, I took the book with me and read it on the voyage, making careful notes. And as I read, I was more and more impressed that through it the Lord was leading me to something—that He had a message in it for His people.

There is enough in this volume to provide material for lengthy meditation. Much of it could be of real value, in this day particularly, to the people of God, and especially to those who have a sense of responsibility for the Lord's interests. For our present consideration we shall only pick out a few of the most vital and essential points; but, when I mention a few of the subjects covered in that volume, you will recognize its very great possibilities. Here are some examples: Supreme

Command; Staff and Personnel—with all the order flowing therefrom; Loyalty Upward to the Top and Downward to the Bottom; Training; Provisioning; Diversity of Function in Unity of Object; Intelligence; Morale; Flexibility; The Great Objective—on the one side, of the Supreme Command, on the other side, of the enemy. The discerning will recognize that these ten points could provide scope for valuable consideration for a long time. If all that were translated and interpreted into spiritual terms, and the Lord's people were in possession of such strategy spiritually, what a tremendously efficient people they would be!

Now, it must be remembered that this is a volume of lessons learned, and that most of these great lessons were learned through defeat. That is, that the terrible story of the first South East Asia campaign—with its devastation, retreat, loss of tens of thousands of lives, and all that goes with that—became history because the vital factors mentioned were either absent or inadequate or in disorder. Surely this provides us with a field for instruction. Should not the people of God and their leaders learn from their defeats and their setbacks at least as quickly and thoroughly?

Higher Direction

We begin with the main thing: 'Supreme Command'. And here the writer of this book uses an expression which I like very much. He calls it: 'Higher Direction'. That is fine! That gets us there! 'Supreme Command'—'Higher Direction'. In that connection there occurs the following sentence: 'The first step towards ultimate victory was the setting up of the Supreme Command, controlling all allied forces of land, sea and air.' What a statement that is when we carry it into the spiritual realm! The turning of a terrible catastrophe, tragedy, defeat into a glorious and consummate victory is here said to have had as its first step—perhaps its main step—the setting up of the Supreme Command. This will resolve itself into several quite distinct matters for our recognition. But this document proves in itself (of course in its own realm, here on the earth), beyond any question or room for doubt, that everything centers in and hangs upon Supreme Command, or Higher Direction.

This was something that seemed to have been overlooked, or had at most been regarded as optional; but now, here is this overwhelming weight of evidence and proof which says that it is absolutely essential. This Higher Direction, this Supreme

Command, is not mere idealism, it is not just something official—it is vital. In this case it was clearly demonstrated that the saving of multitudes of lives, of months and years of time, of honor, liberty, and victory, all hung upon this one matter. Lives were lost, time was thrown away, honor besmirched, liberty sacrificed, victory turned to defeat, and possession turned to loss and nothing, because of the absence of this Supreme Command, this Higher Direction.

And in the light of two thousand years of history, no one will think it exaggeration to say that that is largely the story of the Church: lives, souls, lost; time given away; the honor of the Lord and His Church dragged in the mud. Liberty, victory, fullness?—no, there has not been a great deal of these. And may it not be traceable to this same thing: an undervaluing of, or maladjustment to, the Higher Direction, the Supreme Command? It proved, in the war, to be essential and vital and not open to any option; and in the Church there must be One over all, above all, in all, and through all, and only One in that position.

Mutuality of Understanding

The matter of the necessity for Supreme Command is analyzed, and one thing that comes out of that analysis is this: there must be mutual knowledge and understanding between the Supreme Command and the Forces. Here is a quotation: 'A Supreme Commander, if he is wise, will see that his troops know him'. Much is said about that. The Supreme Commander is not just a name, a figurehead; some remote person somewhere, with his hands upon everything, someone talked about. He is personally known. This book shows how the Supreme Commander made it his business to get down among and be known to his troops, to have a personal touch; he knew his people and they knew him.

This is a simple but profoundly wise statement. What does it carry with it? It carries with it the basic principle that the Lord's first need is to bring us to know Him. Before we can do anything, we must know the Lord. There is no victory without that. Our knowledge of the Lord will determine the measure of our progress in this warfare. The fact is that it is so often for want of that knowledge that we are held up or defeated. To put that the other way round: it is so often just when we come into a new knowledge of the Lord that we go on in a new way of victory. The Lord takes infinite pains to get His people to know Him.

This takes us back into the New Testament. In his letter to the Ephesians—that great battle letter (for such it is)—Paul puts tremendous weight upon the word 'know'. Right at the beginning, he prays: "that ye may know what is the hope of His calling"; "that ye may know... the riches... of His inheritance in the saints"; "that ye may know... the exceeding greatness of His power" (1:18–19). "That ye may know...''! That word 'know' is a governing word in this whole matter of our warfare. Tried warrior that he was, Paul laid the greatest stress on knowing the Lord. "That I may know Him...", he wrote elsewhere (Phil. 3:10). He said that that was far more important than all the other things that are regarded as important by men. He contrasts that knowledge with all that he had had previously—a great world wealth of inheritance. 'But', said he, 'I count all that as nothing—as refuse—that I may know Him'. That made Paul the warrior he was, and from him has come so much for the Church militant.

'The Commander, if he is wise, will see that his own troops know him.' If that could be said of a mortal man here on this earth, our Supreme Commander is no less wise. It is the utmost wisdom—we say it reverently—on the part of the Lord to ensure that our knowledge of Him is ever on the increase.

The Marks of a Supreme Commander

In the next place, let us look at the characteristics required of a Supreme Commander, and their effect upon his forces.

(a) He has a Clearly Defined Objective

Firstly, the Supreme Commander should have a clearly defined objective. We ought to know, from the New Testament, that our Supreme Commander has that; but it is of infinite importance that we know also, with Him, what that clearly defined objective is. That this is not so, accounts for so much of our weakness, resulting in such loss and delay. How many of God's people could express in a few words, from the New Testament, exactly what is the supreme objective of the Lord? Let us challenge ourselves: could we do that? On half a sheet of notepaper, could we put down what the Lord's supreme objective is? If not, we are at a loss, in limitation, in this battle. Think what it would mean if a sufficient number of the Lord's people were solidly bound together by a clear and unquestioning apprehension of the

Lord's ultimate objective! He has made this known to His forces; we have it in His Word: "To make all men see..." (Eph. 3:9). Do you remember what it is they are to see?

(b) He has a Clear Plan for Reaching His Objective

Secondly, the Supreme Commander should have a comprehensive and detailed vision of how he will reach that objective. Our Supreme Commander, without any doubt, has a detailed vision of how He will reach His objective, and therefore we need to be instructed in that in like manner. In other words, we should know, with the Lord, where we are going and what we are after. Are we 'beating about the bush', as we say; are we going round in circles; are we just experimenting? What proportion of all our efforts and expenditure is achieving anything really effective? It is the need of the people of God to be moving together in the integration of a single vision—the vision of the objective and of how God intends to reach it. This is not knowledge beyond our possessing. We have the documents in our hands, if only we would study them and pray for spiritual illumination on this matter. As God's people, we need to be deeply exercised as to how the battle is going. We must first of all know what is God's supreme objective—not just what is incidental or subsidiary; and then, if God has given any light in His Word as to the principles, the ways, the means, by which He intends to reach that end, we must make it our business to know these things also.

(c) He has Command of Adequate Resources

Thirdly, a Supreme Commander must have command of adequate resources to carry the campaign through. That is searching. We need, of course, have no question on that score so far as our Supreme Commander is concerned. We can and must be perfectly at rest on that matter, deeply and quietly and finally assured that He has all the resources at His command for seeing this through. The book to which I have been referring has a long and terrible story to tell of disaster resulting from inadequacy and insufficiency of available resources. There is, as we have said, no question about the adequacy of our Lord's resources, but we surely need to come into the good of that. Again we refer to this great battle document, the Letter to the Ephesians: *"Blessed be the God and Father of our Lord Jesus Christ, Who hath blessed us with every spiritual blessing in the heavenly places in Christ"*

(1:3). Paul had a wonderful apprehension of the resources available for himself and the Church in Christ. It was that apprehension that called forth some of his most joyful superlatives: *"O the depth of the riches" (Rom. 11:33); "the unsearchable riches" (Eph. 3:8);* and others.

A further point of vital importance is this: that, while the Commander may have all these resources at his disposal, it is a terrible thing if something gets in between the Commander and the Army, so that the supplies for the latter are not forthcoming. Of course, that opens up another great subject —that of Communications. But for our warfare there must be no gap whatsoever, whether of doubt, misapprehension, distance, or anything else, between what is there with Him and in Him for us, and what we are knowing of these resources. Again I say that much weakness and defeat, individually and collectively, is due to the needless poverty of God's people, who seem to be drawing upon and enjoying so little of their inheritance. Many do not know of the resources available. No wonder the enemy is having so much of his own way!

(d) He has the Confidence of His Forces

Fourthly, the Commander must have—'A staff and Army having implicit confidence in him, and willing to subordinate all personal and sectional considerations to him—absolute confidence in his judgment, his wisdom, his generalship, even when his ways are not understood.' If men can talk like that about one another, when stating the essentials of a victorious campaign on this earth level, surely that is something that we ought to understand and carry over into the spiritual—'A staff' (what is the spiritual equivalent of this?) 'and Army, having implicit confidence in the Supreme Command, in His understanding, in His wisdom, in His judgment, in His generalship, even when His ways are not understood.'

Sometimes He commands and His commands are difficult to understand; sometimes His ways are really "past finding out"; sometimes it almost seems that what He is doing, or essaying to do, will prove completely disastrous. Nevertheless, when we cannot or do not understand, when His ways run counter to our best natural judgment, then is the test: have we implicit confidence in Him? When He seems to be doing nothing, when He seems to be absent from the field, when His ways are so strange and mysterious, have we implicit confidence in His judgment, His wisdom? It is a test, is it not?

But remember again, that the whole campaign, both in its first phase of disaster and defeat and in its second phase of glorious full victory, hung upon that—a willingness in all concerned to subordinate all personal and sectional interests to the Supreme Command and give him unquestioned leadership. And a similar unquestioned devotion on our part is surely called for. Nothing could serve the enemy's purposes better than for us to have a question about our Commander's leadership, a doubt about His generalship, His wisdom; that would just sabotage the whole campaign. They are words easily said, perhaps, but that is the subtlety of the battle we are in. Very often the battle has to be won inwardly before it can be won outwardly, and the inward battle circles around this question of implicit confidence in our Lord, unquestioning devotion to Him, the subduing of everything to His Lordship. Until we are settled on this point, we are a weakness in the Army, and we shall not be in the way of victory.

(e) He has the Loyalty of His Forces

Fifth, the Supreme Commander must have the absolute loyalty of all concerned. Much is made of that. Moreover, there must be not only loyalty to the Supreme Command, but loyalty also to all appointed by the Supreme Command, and loyalty amongst all ranks—loyalty, in fact, to the whole 'outfit'. What a vital matter this is! May not the explanation of a great deal of painful history be traced to some measure of disloyalty on our part—if not to our Lord, then to one another, to the Lord's people? There needs to be a new loyalty all round, upward and downward, and a committal to the Lord's supreme purpose: which means that anybody and everybody in that purpose is our comrade, and we are committed to him and to her.

The Spiritual Parallel and Application

Now these five characteristics of a Commander, embodying as they do the great strategic principles of this campaign, must be interpreted and translated into spiritual strategy. There must be the supreme value of a focal point of confidence and co-ordination. This is exactly what was established in the resurrection, ascension, and exaltation of the Lord Jesus: "...made Him to sit at His right hand... far above all rule, and authority... and every name that is named" (Eph. 1:20–21). There is the Supreme Command, the Higher Direction, the focal point of all confidence and co-ordination. Paul said much about this matter of co-ordination in the Head. Everything is "fitly framed"; every joint 'makes supply' (Eph. 4:16); everything works harmoniously together and makes its contribution, when it is focused in the Head, and when He is "Head over all things to the church" (Eph. 1:22–23). I know I have changed the metaphor from the Army to the Body, but the principle is the same.

But although it was in the ascension and exaltation of the Lord Jesus that this focal point of all confidence and relatedness was established, it only came into operation on the day of Pentecost. The ascension and exaltation of Jesus is, in fact, the explanation of the presence of the Holy Spirit (John 7:39). Pentecost, after all, is the counterpart of Joshua's experience before Jericho. Joshua, lifting up his eyes, saw a man standing with his sword drawn, and he "went unto him, and said unto him, 'Art thou for us, or for our adversaries?' And he said, 'Nay; but as captain of the host of the Lord am I now come' " (Josh. 5:13–14). Joshua prostrated himself, took off his shoes, and worshipped—he went down before that One. That represents Pentecost in its outworking. The Captain of the hosts of the Lord has come to take over. The Holy Spirit is here in the Name and function of the exalted Lord. Which raises the whole question of how far the Church and every individual—the Army and every member of it—is under that one government of the Holy Spirit. That, and that only, will ensure a victorious campaign, a turning of defeat into victory.

The Challenge of 'The Supreme Command'

This matter of the Lord being in His place has a very wide application. There are quite a number of people who recognize and accept the leadership of the Lord Jesus, in name and phraseology and profession, but who in themselves are a definite contradiction to it. There are quite a lot of 'free-lances' in this war—people moving on their own in an unrelated way—who strongly, yes, vehemently declare, 'Jesus is Lord': but, if they only knew their own hearts, they are lord of their lives, of their ways; their likes and dislikes and preferences govern. Yes, there are those who, while acclaiming Jesus 'Lord' and speaking about 'surrender' (a great word, 'surrender'!), are nevertheless strong objectors to any kind of discipline, any kind of government, control or direction. They repudiate all that sort of thing; they say: 'I am free in the Lord!' The Lord's own appointed under-officers are either ignored or insulted, or at least not honored.

This is just playing into the hands of the enemy. All wisdom is against it, and we have a mighty weight of evidence in the Word of God that it is not God's mind. God has, first of all, His Supreme Command, His Higher Direction, but He has also under that Command His 'subordinate staff', if we may use the term—His ordered system of delegated spiritual responsibility; and this must be recognized. If it is not, the Army is held up, and the enemy is given just what he wants. Moreover, there is complete confusion and frustration in the ranks.

There are, on the other hand, those people who have put legalism in the place of the Holy Spirit, who have substituted legality for light and love, made it the Supreme Command, constituted a system the final authority. As we know, Paul encountered this legalism in the battle; and, if we may judge from the letter to the Galatians, it was this that drew out his fighting spirit more than anything else. *'Let him be anathema! I repeat: Let him he anathema!' (Gal. 1:8–9).* This was directed against anyone who would put a system in the place of the Holy Spirit.

Others are like the Corinthians who, in their spiritual disorder and weakness and defeat, were actuated solely by natural preferences, natural judgment and natural choices amongst men and things. Their selection and allegiance is according to human thoughts and judgments, likes and dislikes. If such considerations get their way, 'Corinthian' conditions will prevail. And let us remember that Paul headed up the whole Corinthian situation into the threat of a repetition of what happened to Israel in the wilderness, with all those armies of the first generation (1 Cor. 10:1–11). They perished there; 'and', says Paul 'that is the way you are going, unless you see to this one thing, that Jesus Christ is Lord. You must not be governed by your own preferences, your likes and your dislikes, your judgments and your choices. Unless you give the Holy Spirit His rightful place, in charge of your soul with all its activities, that is the end to which you will come—you will perish in the wilderness!'

Our Warfare

May the Lord find us recognizing the "Supreme Command": obedient to Him, and loyal both to Him and to one another.

The Twofold Main Objective

*"For though we walk in the flesh, we do not war according to the
flesh (for the weapons of our warfare are not of the flesh, but
mighty before God to the casting down of strong-holds); casting
down imaginations, and every high thing that is exalted against the
knowledge of God, and bringing every thought into captivity to the
obedience of Christ" (2 Corinthians 10:3–5).*

We pass now to the next of the vital things in the warfare
—The Twofold Main Objective: the twofold main objective
of God, the twofold main objective of the enemy. This great
campaign has two aspects: one is primary; the other is

secondary. One is the final supreme issue; the other is the means or instrument for its attainment. We shall consider both of these things, but mainly the second.

First of all, the supreme objective of God—and therefore of Satan—in its primary aspect, may be summed up in what is meant by 'the Throne'. The rights, the claims, and the aims of the Throne; the sphere and range of its influence; the honor that is bound up with it; the government that it implies; the prosperity and well-being of the people over whom it is set: all these things go to make up what is meant by the Throne. That, supremely and finally, is God's objective. All those things are but aspects of God's interests and activities and concern in this great campaign. The Throne, with all that meaning, is involved in this tremendous conflict.

It is, therefore, easy to see what is the enemy's objective: it is the reverse or contrary of what we have just stated. He aims at the repudiation of the rights and claims and interests of that Throne; the curtailment, and, if possible, the complete removal, of the influence of that Throne; the depriving of the people under it of their prosperity and wellbeing. All this is what the enemy is set upon; and his consummate object, along all those lines, is himself to take over everything—even the very Throne itself.

In making these statements, I am, of course, keeping close to the Scriptures and close to history. We ought to realize what it is that we are involved in and what we are up against.

The Church the Instrument of the Throne

With that brief word on the primary aspect of the supreme objective, we pass to what I have called the secondary aspect: but it is only secondary in that it is dependent upon the primary. This—the means for the attainment of the supreme objective—is the instrument in which all those features and factors of the Throne are vested, to which they are committed and entrusted. In order to repudiate the rights, the claims, and the interests of the Throne; to bring dishonor and reproach upon it; to curtail or wipe out the sphere of its influence; to rob its subjects of their prosperity and well-being; in order to do all this, the enemy must destroy or put out of action the whole force in the field—the vehicle and means of operation of that Throne, the instrumentality of its effectiveness. That vehicle is the Church. It is to the Church that all those interests of the Throne are committed; it is in the Church that they are vested.

But let us not consider that word 'Church' objectively: let us bring it right to ourselves, and apply every word personally. In this matter we need not fear that we shall be too subjective, too self-occupied or introspective. Our conception of 'the Church' must not be of something vague or mystical. Wherever even two or three are gathered into the Name, there is the Church in real, though minute, representation, and everything begins there. And so it is that these tremendous things in relation to the Throne, as the supreme and ultimate objective of God and the enemy, are focused upon us as a part of the Church.

The Groaning of the Creation Related to the Church

There is a sense in which it can be said that all the trouble centers in the Church. Like the prophets, one of whom was addressed as the "troubler of Israel" (1 Kings 18:17), the Church is the 'troubler', not only of Israel, but of all the nations and of the kingdom of Satan. Even in our own day, there is a great deal that corresponds to those tremendous convulsions in Egypt that led up to the ejection of Israel. That is the explanation of much that is taking place in the nations today. Convulsions in the nations—what for? Well, Paul says that "the whole creation groaneth and travaileth"—why? It is waiting for "the revealing of the sons of God" (Rom. 8:22, 19). It is toward the birth, the manifestation, the precipitation, of that which God has ultimately in view, that there are these convulsions in the nations. That may seem a big thing to say, and indeed, if we had not Bible ground for saying it, we should be saying something too big. But all those convulsions in Egypt were because of a people in their midst who had to be got out—and the power behind that kingdom was not prepared to let them out! The hierarchy of wicked spirits that were the real rulers of the land of Egypt did not want that people out, because they knew that the emancipation of Israel would constitute the greatest possible menace to their hold upon Egypt and other nations of the earth.

Centuries later, when Israel was again in captivity, there were upheavals in Babylon. Through the prophet the Lord said: "I have sent to Babylon, and will bring down all their nobles" (Isa. 43:14, marg.)—what for? To get the People out. Convulsions in Babylon! And there are plenty of convulsions in the nations of the world just now. I believe that the trouble is largely because of the Church. Once the Church is extricated and out, while there will be disintegration, judgment and so on, Satan will breathe more freely here. But, whether this be a right interpretation or not concerning national and international upheavals and tumults—and I think it is—there is no question whatever as to whether or not it is true about the kingdom of Satan. The cause of the trouble, disturbance and upheaval there is this other force that is in the field. It is the troubler.

The Conflict Focused upon a True Expression of Christ

Now, immediately there is a movement towards the practical expression of anything approximating to the Church as it is revealed in the New Testament—especially as revealed in such fullness through the Letters of the Apostle Paul—disturbances take place which are more than human, for which there seems to be no rational explanation. This should give food for thought. It is profoundly significant that no comparable spiritual disturbance arises when Christianity is anything short of this. There may be a presentation of doctrine without organic expression: that does not worry Satan very much. We may be orthodox and as sound as it is possible to be, and still not meet the full force of Satan's objection. But let an organic expression of the Church for practical purposes be brought into view, and you will find trouble coming from everywhere and nowhere!

Again, when Christianity is a formal, ecclesiastical system, without spiritual power, Satan does not trouble either himself or it one little bit. When Christianity is a mystical, aesthetic, artistic, soulish imitation of spirituality, Satan is not at all troubled—rather very pleased. He is delighted when mysticism is interpreted as spirituality, and multitudes are held in the illusion. When there is profession without organic reality, there is no trouble. When there is but a name, a title, a designation, without correspondence to the Divine pattern, it is left to go on its way unchallenged. When there is an organization, an institution, without a heavenly nature and spiritual character, its course is more or less unchecked. But let the Lord bring into view something that really sets forth Christ corporately, and then there is trouble—trouble, such as we have said, that cannot be explained along any natural, human lines at all.

The enemy is, in fact, bitterly opposed to any real, living, organic expression of Christ in his territory. For such an expression really represents the Throne of God, in effect and in impact, and therefore there will be trouble. The forces of Satan in any and every way are set against the realization of that. From apostolic times until now, there never was an expression, however small, of the Church in its heavenly, spiritual and eternal character, that was not the object of the most determined and many sided effort of Satan to destroy it. There is a great deal of history bound up in that statement. This is, after all, just the meaning of Ephesians 6:12 and onward, is it not? "Our wrestling is not against flesh and blood, but against the principalities... powers... world- rulers of this darkness... spiritual hosts of wickedness in the heavenly places." But long before Paul wrote those words, Paul's Master, the Lord Jesus Himself, had spoken about this great Satanic opposition. He spoke of "the gates of Hades"— which I understand to mean 'the councils of death' —as being active with the determination to prevail against the Church.

Now it would be far too big a matter for us to try to arrange the strategies and tactics of the enemy in this connection. But let us note two things.

The Twofold Main Objective

The first is that the Throne—with all that it implies—is most closely affected by the representation of Christ—whether good, or bad—that is found in the Church; that is, according to whether Christ is, in fact, represented or misrepresented. The Throne is affected more directly and immediately by the Church than by anything else. That is the fact.

Secondly, we need always to remember that secondary causes are not primary causes. Would that we might be more alive and alert to that! We are caught almost every time on that matter. Things happen: people behave in such and such a way; circumstances arise; there is strain, tumult, tension and what not; and we attribute everything to the secondary cause—to the person or the persons concerned, to the circumstances, the conditions, or whatever it might be. We do not go straight to the first cause. We fail to recognize that behind everything is this sinister force; behind that person's behavior there is something more; behind all this there is something at work with no less an objective than the undermining of that Throne—its honor, its glory, its range and sphere of influence, its rights and its claims and the wellbeing of its people. In many a little, seemingly casual, 'happening', it is nothing less than that which is involved: but we take it on as something in itself, and wrongly make the secondary cause the first.

In the previous chapter I said that there are many things that we should attribute to our own foolishness, rather than to the Devil. But there is this other realm, and lest you think I am exaggerating, let me bring you to the Word. Some of these so called secondary causes—failure to recognize which leads to the defeat of the Church, or the setback of the Army—are actually found in this letter to the Ephesians, the great warfare letter of the Church.

'Ephesians'—The Warfare Letter

"The Exceeding Greatness of the Revelation"

In the three great chapters at the beginning of this letter, we have presented the Church of God; that marvelous vessel, that Divine masterpiece, born in the counsels of God in eternity past. I fear that the chapter divisions sometimes prevent us from recognizing the continuity, the unity of the whole document, and from passing naturally from one stage to another. But here we have the presentation of this great thing—it is as it were brought out from eternity and shown to us. And this presentation, comprehended in a few hundred words of human language, is something which for well-nigh twenty centuries has defeated and defied every attempt to fathom it, and today it is drawing out and extending men more than ever before. That is not exaggeration. Can you fathom it? Look again at some of the shortest sentences in those first three chapters—they will defeat you!

Now, the subject matter contained in the second half (chapters 4–6) of the letter arranges itself into four sections, the first two short, the last two long. Whilst we shall review them very briefly, let us not fail to apply them.

(a) "Walking Worthily of the Calling"

Paul, having thus presented the Church, now, by a perfectly natural movement, passes to a consideration of the practical consequences. His opening words are full of challenge and test. *"I... beseech you to walk worthily of the calling wherewith ye were called, with all lowliness and meekness, with patience, forbearing one another in love, eager to maintain the unity of the Spirit..." (Eph. 4:1–3; vs. 3 R.S.V.).* Now, these are things that are directly related to certain very common 'secondary causes'. But this whole immense purpose, that has been unveiled, divulged, as out from eternity, rests for its true expression, for the proof that it is no mere vision, no mere idea or ideal, but a reality—it all rests upon our 'walking worthily'. It rests upon our walk. Everything depends upon our lowliness, meekness, patience, our forbearing one another in love, our eagerness to keep the unity. Does that challenge us? But those are our spiritual weapons in the field, and much grace and faith is needed if they are to be used effectively.

Oh, the provocations, the annoyances, the irritations!—all that comes upon us in the course of a day to make our life a contradiction and our walk unworthy! The challenge to lowliness! The snare of self-assertiveness, loudness, occupying the limelight, bringing ourselves into view, drawing attention to ourselves, wanting people to take note of us—all that and a thousand other things contrary to lowliness and meekness! "With patience, forbearing one another, giving diligence to keep the unity"—so our Revised Version; the Revised Standard Version has: "eager to maintain the unity"—eager, eager to maintain the unity! Ah, that is a battle, a tremendous battle, a desperate part of the conflict. The enemy is particularly persistent and persevering with things like these, because they make a caricature of the Church, and they touch the Throne.

But every one of those things can be carried into the realm of what we call 'secondary causes'. 'But he did so and so... she said so and so... and I got upset... and I have a right to be upset!' That is looking at things as they appear on the surface, instead of looking right through the things and seeing something else. Ah, yes; if we look deeper, we shall find that there is a primary cause. Often the very timing of the thing proves that—it is so sinister and so uncanny. Or a consideration of where the attack comes from, or the why of it, may reveal its true source. But we are not always alive to that. We get caught in the thing and defeated, and all our wonderful conceptions of this marvelous Church count for nothing—they just go to pieces.

(b) "The Unity of the Faith"

We turn to the second section, chapter 4:4–6. Here, quite briefly, the thing challenged is the peril of making something extra to Christ the basis of unity. "There is... one Lord, one faith, one baptism, one God and Father of all". That is the basis of unity. But it is possible to make a division by means of that, if you are so minded. I have heard people ask, 'What does the "one baptism" mean?' Some say: 'Of course it means the baptism of the Holy Spirit', and others: 'Of course it means the baptism of water'—and at once there is a division on the very fundamentals of unity! I do not think that either of those interpretations necessarily applies here. What it does mean, I believe, is this: that 'we were all baptized in one Spirit into one Body' (1 Cor. 12:13), and the "one baptism" is baptism into Christ. You can say that it is by the Holy Spirit, if you like. I challenge you to say that it is by water. No one is baptized into Christ by water. They may testify to baptism into Christ by means of water, but that is another thing. The one baptism is that, when we believed, we were all baptized in one Spirit into one Body.

The issue, then, is: Are you in Christ? Have you been baptized into Christ? That is fundamental to unity. If we make something more to be a basis of unity, then we split the unity, we destroy it, we contradict the truth of the oneness. This foundation is sufficient. If we knew all that is included in this "one Lord, one faith, one baptism, one God and Father", we should have enough. If we live according to that, we take a lot of ground from under the enemy. Immediately we begin to add to that, as the basis of unity, then we begin to give the whole position away. Our special interpretations and teachings and doctrines have no value whatsoever as a basis of unity. All that matters is the foundation, and that is sufficient.

(c) Holiness of Life

The third section, chapter 4:17—5:20, is a long section, containing a great many things and covering much ground. But if you read the section through, you will find that it all amounts to this: holiness of living, personally and relatedly. And remember that the enemy is against that. He triumphed in the greater part of the churches in Asia along that line. The chief thing that the Lord had to lay at their door, in His messages through the Apostle John, was corruption, defilement, wrongness in the moral life. Paul, here, has much to say on this matter of holiness, first in ourselves individually and then between us and others. For if the enemy can touch us and spoil us on that ground, he has struck at the Throne: he has brought reproach upon it, he has limited the sphere of its influence, he has robbed us and others of our inheritance. And that is searching!

(d) Human Relationships

Finally we have the fourth section: chapter 5:21—6:9. This section deals, mainly, with domestic relationships— husbands to wives; wives to husbands; children to parents; parents to children; servants to masters; masters to servants. And these relationships present peculiarly good opportunities for enemy activity. But here, again, we are so insensible to reality that we habitually make these secondary causes the primary ones. How often it is that provocations and strains and difficulties in these family and social relationships have the effect of putting us spiritually right out of action, of crippling or even nullifying our spiritual life. And, again, these things often come up in such an uncanny way. Can we not learn this lesson from our defeats? So often the enemy comes along, either through the wife or the husband, in relation to something of very great spiritual interest that is about to emerge. We may know nothing of this—but he knows! The same thing may happen with regard to the children; the Devil can play many tricks through them.

So the whole range of these relationships is brought in here. The point is: we must not always lose our heads and straightaway blame the persons concerned. If we do, we have lost the battle. Let us first of all, if opportunity offers, go quietly away and say: 'Now, what is the enemy up to—what is he after? There is probably something more here than just this upset, however real and justified it may seem. It is quite true that this and that has happened; it is not imagination: but is this the beginning and the end of it? Cannot this be completely destroyed from behind? Cannot this be dealt with at Headquarters?' You see what I mean. On a hasty and superficial view, we might take all these things for primary causes. But quiet and prayerful reflection will enable us to recognize them as, in all probability, only secondary ones. We must not make secondary causes the criterion, but must get behind them to the hidden primary cause—in this case the activity of the great enemy.

Revelation and Warfare Related

Now you will notice that the four passages, or sections, that we have just considered are placed between Paul's mighty unveiling and presentation of the Church and his great exposé of the spiritual warfare over it. A significant position! Here is this matchless thought of God, the Church, presented. Here, at the other end, is the warfare with myriads of evil spirits. And, sandwiched right in between, we find husband and wife, and wife and husband; children and parents, and so on. Do you protest that there is no connection!? I submit, in reply, that the "therefore" of chapter 4, verse 1, holds this middle section, concerning our conduct and behavior, in direct relation to the preceding revelation; saying in effect: 'Therefore, unless you watch these relationships, all that revelation counts for nothing!'

And the "Finally" of chapter 6 (which word does not mean 'Last of all'; it means 'Now, taking everything up from this point onward', 'Gathering everything up to go on')—that "Finally" gathers into the battle both the revelation and the conduct. "Finally, be strong in the Lord... For our wrestling..." This is all part of a tremendous fight. It is as much a part of spiritual warfare to deal with all the things which you may regard as the trivial commonplaces of everyday life—as much a part of the great spiritual warfare and the great issue of the Throne, as to be right out in the naked battle with the enemy himself.

In closing, we note that all this that we have seen carries with it certain serious implications. It says this, to begin with: that the holding of the doctrine of the Church, as in Ephesians

1–3, without corresponding life and walk, may sabotage the whole issue. We may have the conception of the Church—wonderful terms, wonderful ideas; we may talk endlessly about it, because it is so marvelous, so fascinating—but is it working? Is it really working? Are we truly in it? The answer will only be found in our daily walk and conduct, in all the so called 'commonplace' relationships that we have mentioned. That is the answer. It is really a matter of how much we are in this with all that we are and all that we have.

I remember hearing Dr. Campbell Morgan make a very challenging remark. He said: 'Allow me an impossible proposition: Supposing Christ is to be defeated, what do you stand to lose? How much of you is invested in this matter? Do you stand to lose everything if Christ is defeated?' Yes, it is an impossible proposition, because He never can be defeated. But supposing that in some way or other He is defeated in us, what do we stand to lose?

At The Heart of the Conflict is the Throne

Again, to divorce all these practical matters from the interests of the Church and from spiritual conflict is to have no dynamic with which to deal with them. Do you grasp that?

If you cannot deal with these domestic situations effectively: if you are just struggling with them—'he is such an awkward husband', 'she is such a difficult wife', 'those children are such a handful'—if you are struggling to cope with them, and you know that you are not getting very far, may it not, after all, be a Church matter, that you have not an adequate background for dealing with the situations? May it not be that you are trying to deal with it as something in itself, instead of bringing it into relation with the Lord's testimony? that you are not recognizing that this discord, this disagreement between you and your husband or your wife touches the Throne, touches the Lord's honor, and must be dealt with on no lesser ground than that? It is not merely a matter of settling our little domestic problem—we must have a dynamic for dealing with situations in general. And it may be that, when we bring these things into the right realm, recognizing that they are a part of the great spiritual conflict in which the Throne is involved, we shall find things happening surprisingly.

But we come back at length to where we started. Beyond and above all this detail, the dominant issue is that of the Throne: its honor and glory; its sphere and range of influence;

the rights and claims and interests of the Throne, and the wellbeing of the people under it. Everything comes back to that, for that is the object of the conflict. In our homes, and in our local companies, let us cease to criticize, to judge, to condemn, looking at one another, and laying the blame at the door of things and people; and let us see if our problem ought not to be dealt with from behind. And let the Church deal with it so, in any locality. Let the Church face the situation squarely: 'Look here, the Lord's Throne and the Lord's honor are touched by this. We believe that God raised up this instrument and vessel: if so, it was in relation to the Throne. It is necessary, therefore, that this vessel be a true representation of the Church, according to the Word of God; and hence we realize that all Hell will be out to spoil it, to mar it, to wreck it, to destroy it.'

Why is this so? Not because the enemy cares anything about you or me, as individuals, or about any little local group or company, as something in itself; but he has his eye on that Throne, and our situation—either in the home or in the church—is touching that. Let us adjust to this reality—for it is all here in the Word, it is true; let us deal with matters in that way. Let our attitude be: 'This situation must not proceed any further; because of what is involved, it must not remain another day. The enemy must at all costs be spoiled in this!'

Morale

"Then Jerubbaal, who is Gideon, and all the people that were with him, rose up early, and encamped beside the spring of Harod: and the camp of Midian was on the north side of them, by the hill of Moreh, in the valley. And the Lord said unto Gideon, The people that are with thee are too many for Me to give the Midianites into their hand, lest Israel vaunt themselves against Me, saying, Mine own hand hath saved me. Now therefore proclaim in the ears of the people, saying, Whosoever is fearful and trembling, let him return and depart from mount Gilead. And there returned of the people twenty and two thousand; and there remained ten thousand. And the Lord said unto Gideon, The people are yet too many; bring them down unto the water, and I will try them for thee there: and it shall be, that of whom I say unto thee, This shall go with thee, the same shall go with thee; and of whomsoever I say unto thee, This shall not go with thee, the same shall not go. So he brought down the people unto the water: and the Lord said unto Gideon, Every one that lappeth of the water with his tongue, as a dog lappeth, him shalt thou set by himself; likewise every one that boweth down upon his knees to drink. And the number of them that lapped, putting their hand to their mouth, was three hundred men: but all the rest of the people bowed down upon their knees to drink water. And the Lord said unto Gideon, By the three hundred men that lapped will I save you, and deliver the Midianites into thy hand; and let all the people go every man unto his place" (Judges 7:1–7; R.S.V.).

One of the most important aspects of the whole subject treated in our book, *Defeat into Victory*, was the question of 'Morale'. A very great deal of space is given in that record to this matter of morale: for its lack on some occasions, and its collapse on others, were responsible for what was little less than a complete rout; conversely, its recovery played a very large part in the glorious consummation.

The Reducing of Gideon's Army

That word 'morale', of course, lies right at the heart of the story of Gideon. It sums up the whole matter, does it not? First of all, there is an elimination of everyone who is fearful and trembling; in the second stage, everyone who has interests which are personal and which, standing to suffer, would cause the breakdown of morale, is bidden to go home. This great reducing movement was called for by the Lord in order to get a certain quality. Of course, as regards numbers, this is no kind of argument either for one thing or the other: it is not an argument for large numbers and it is not an argument for small numbers. Nor, let us be clear, has this anything to do with salvation. The redeemed are to be 'a great multitude which no man can number' (Rev. 7:9). "The Lord is... longsuffering... not wishing that any should perish, but that all should come to repentance" (2 Pet. 3:9). The Lord has no reservations in that sphere; He never says that that number is too great. But here it is a question of service—specific service and responsibility for the interests of the Lord amongst His own people. It is a matter of the Lord's honor.

To get the real value of this story, we need to remember the situation which obtained at that time amongst the people of God. For the issue was indeed the honor of the Name of the Lord, as deposited with His own people; and for the deliverance of that Name from reproach and dishonor among His people a certain quality of fighting force is required. That is the heart of the story, and that is what we are considering at this point.

The Challenge of Active Service

Now before we go further with the matter of morale, may I come back to the general matter of our warfare. We may have had much teaching on various aspects of Divine truth and revelation, such as the Church, the Body of Christ, and other matters, and it may be that the teaching has not been without value—it may even have been quite profitable. But I wonder whether we have made enough of this matter of our being, as the Lord's people, really on a war footing. Has it really come home to us that we, the people of God, are supposed to be in the field under war conditions? Is there the mentality and consciousness in every section and in every individual that we are in a great campaign; that there is no letup in this matter, and that we are in it up to the hilt? There may be, and indeed often is, a real gap between our teaching, instruction, information, on the subject of Christian soldiering, and the assured conviction of being actually in a war—on active service. So many of the Lord's people listen to the teaching, and are interested in it, but they are not really in the fight, not really counting in the battle. To sing 'Onward, Christian Soldiers!' and to do no fighting, is naïve.

Surely, at such a time as this, the Lord would challenge us all, young and old alike: 'Are you really alive to the fact that you are out in active warfare, in a great campaign? that you are a part of something tremendous that is going on in this universe, and that you have a personal and quite definite place in it?' It is a matter of urgency that this should be brought home to us definitely and clearly. It may be that much of our defeat, many of the casualties amongst us, are largely due to the fact that we have not been on the war path with the enemy: we have been letting him have his way far too much, we have been giving him ground, we have been letting him play around with us and do as he likes. If only we had been standing on our feet in this matter, perhaps some casualties might have been avoided. We have just accepted circumstances—including physical weaknesses—as unrelated things in themselves, instead of standing up and at least raising the question: 'How much is there of the enemy behind this?' Of course, it may not be that in every case of physical or other limitation the enemy is having the ascendancy, but in a great many cases he is, and the way of deliverance is to recognize that we must "lay hold on eternal life" and "fight the good fight of faith" (1 Tim. 6:12, A.V.). "Lay hold on eternal life"!

The Foundations of Morale

Now, on this matter of morale, I want to quote an excellent passage from the book of which I have spoken. Says the writer, the great Field Marshal who made this report: 'Morale is a state of mind, it is that intangible force which will move a whole group of men to give their last ounce to achieve something without counting the cost to themselves, that makes them feel that they are part of something greater than themselves. If they are to feel that, their morale—if it is to endure, and the essence of morale is that it should endure—their morale must have certain foundations. These foundations are spiritual, intellectual, material, and that is the order of their importance. Spiritual first, because only spiritual foundations can stand the real strain.' (Is that not fine? Of course there may be varying conceptions of the meaning of the word 'spiritual', but when one interprets this in the realm of heavenly things, the principle is so sound, the wisdom so profound.) 'Intellectual next, because men are swayed by reason as well as feeling. Material last—important but last—because the very highest kinds of morale are often when men's material conditions are at their lowest.' (What a great deal of spiritual profit could be drawn from that!)

He goes on to say: 'I remember sitting down in my office and tabulating these foundations something like this':

1. *The Spiritual:*
    a. *There must be a great and noble object;*
    b. *Its achievement must be absolutely vital;*
    c. *The method of its achievement must be active, aggressive;*
    d. *The man must feel that what he is and what he does matters directly towards the attainment of the object.*

(How full that is of vital and necessary lessons when translated into the realm of things heavenly!)

2. *The Intellectual:*

    a. *He must be convinced in his mind that the object can be attained' (that is searching!);*

    b. *He must see, too, that the organization to which he belongs, and which is striving to obtain the object, is sound and efficient;*

(Perhaps we could interpret that as meaning that we must believe in our cause and recognize the adequacy of the Church's spiritual equipment for gaining the object in view.)

    c. *He must have confidence in his leaders and know that, whatever dangers and hardships he is called upon to suffer, his life will not be thrown away for nothing.*

3. *The Material:*

    a. *The man must feel that he will get a fair deal from his commander and from the Army;*

(We have no fear about getting a fair deal from our Commander! We know He will give us a fair deal. But perhaps we cannot always be so certain of getting a fair deal from the Army, either individually or as a

whole. To be certain of the support of the rest of the Army is an important factor in morale.)

    b. He must, as far as possible, be given the best weapons and equipment for his task;

(That throws us back, does it not, upon the responsibility of 'under shepherds' to give instruction in "the whole counsel of God", that the Church may be 'thoroughly furnished' for her warfare?)

    c. His working conditions must be made as good as can be.

Having thus analyzed and summarized what he means by foundations of morale, the writer next adds a classic sentence, which I have doubly underlined. Note, this is a Field Marshal of the Army speaking. He dares to say:

'The Christian religion is above all others a source of that enduring courage which is the most valued of all the components of morale'!

And the book contains much more like that. This matter of morale is of the greatest importance. It was against the possible lack or breakdown of such morale that the Lord took those very serious precautions with Gideon; when He said: "By the three hundred men that lapped will I save you, and deliver the Midianites into thine hand" (Judges 7:7).

The Enemy's Assaults upon Morale

Now, if we think about it for a few moments, we cannot fail to realize what a great deal our New Testament has to say about morale. For, after all, such admonitions and entreaties as: "Be strong in the grace that is in Christ Jesus" (2 Tim. 2:1); "Be strong in the Lord, and in the strength of His might" (Eph. 6:10); "Quit you like men, be strong" (1 Cor. 16:13); all such exhortations have to do with this strategic matter of spiritual morale—spiritual stamina to go on and to keep going on. I want to stress the importance that the Lord attaches to this. Let me refer for a moment to what we were saying in the previous chapter. The great objective of the enemy is to bring reproach upon the Crown, upon the Throne; to repudiate its rights, its claims, its interests; to rob the people of the Crown, of their heritage. And if that is to be met and countered and overcome, this matter of spiritual stamina that we are calling 'morale' is of tremendous importance.

The writer from whom we are quoting makes some sorry comparisons of conditions in the opposing sides at the beginning of the campaign. Speaking about the enemy's morale, he says that for a long time it was almost impossible to break it, and he puts it down to one thing. He says: 'The enemy fought his battle as though upon every individual there rested the whole interest, the whole issue. For instance, if 500 men were told off to hold a position, 'we had to kill 495 before we got that position and the remaining five killed themselves. Not one man would surrender.' In every individual there was this consciousness that the whole war issue rested upon him and his life: he was in this thing without any reserve or question, or other interest. That was the secret of his morale, and that lies behind, on the one hand, the great story of the enemy's long continued victory, and, on the other hand, our defeat.

That is the key to the whole matter, is it not? "Whosoever is fearful and trembling..." Why should we be fearful and trembling—why? Why should we be afraid? Is there something in our life for which we care more than for this great issue—that of the Throne and the Crown, the government and our fellow countrymen's heritage of heavenly citizenship? Is there something that to us is of greater importance? Then that is the root of the fear and trembling. The very presence of fear indicates that there is some other interest. If the interests and honor of the Throne are our only concern, it means that all other things have been set aside and we are in this battle to the death. That, clearly, defines the strength of morale in the story of Gideon; these people had no alternatives, no secondary considerations.

Says our writer: 'The fighting soldier facing such an enemy must see that what he does, whether he is brave or craven, matters to all his comrades, and directly influences the result of the whole battle.' It is this personal aspect to which everything is headed up in this seventh chapter of the Book of Judges. This is clearly brought out in the more modern translation given in the Revised Standard Version: "He of whom I say to you, 'This man shall go with you,' shall go with you; and any of whom I say to you, 'This man shall not go with you,' shall not go" (vs. 4). God was dealing with thousands, yet He would not handle them as it were 'in bulk'. He dealt with them man by man; He made it a personal matter with each man individually. And so it was—'This man shall go with you...', and, 'This man shall not go with you...' The whole thing was made personal.

The Corporate Effect of Morale

But—"none of us liveth to himself, and none dieth to himself" (Rom. 14:7). That is to say, the way you and I individually stand up in this battle affects the whole issue. Did we but believe it, what a wonderful source of support and strength this is! But whether we believe it or not, that is a statement of fact. It is recognized in the natural world, and it is just as true, if not more so, in the spiritual realm. "Now we live, if ye stand fast in the Lord"! (1 Thess. 3:8). Your behavior and mine in the battle—whether we stand up or give up—profoundly affects other people. It surely does! We need to lay hold of that and to say: 'The issue, after all, does not begin and end with me. My conduct, my spirit, my attitude affects others. If I am weakening in the fight; if I am an unreliable soldier; if I cannot be trusted from one day to another as to how I shall be and where I shall be: if I am like that, it affects the whole situation. It is a cause of weakness in the whole corporate Body, in the whole constitution.' It must be our constant motive for girding ourselves and being strong, that our brothers and sisters need us so—the whole battle needs us to be like that. We dare not be weak and give up, for in this business we just cannot isolate ourselves.

The Lord was acting on this ground with Gideon's army. He said, in effect: 'If I were to allow any one man, fearful and trembling, to come into this undertaking, he would affect all the others, and I cannot afford that: let every such man go. And if I allowed any man to come in who had personal interests to serve, whose natural pride and conceit would take some glory to himself, that would be disastrous for the whole issue: let all such go home. The men who are to be here, who are to be the instrument of this deliverance, must be men who have been reduced to sheer, intrinsic worth.' That, surely, explains much of the Lord's dealings with us—reducing, emptying, weakening, breaking down, scattering. What is God doing? Just making way for intrinsic values, the values which are to be found when our objective is the Lord, and only the Lord. The issue for us must be the Lord—His glory, His honor.

That, in a few words, is morale. Much more could, of course, be said on this vital matter. Let me close with one other short extract. Says the writer: 'We had the advantage of our enemies in that our cause was based on real, not false, spiritual values. We fought only because the powers of evil (what a phrase!) had attacked those real spiritual values.'

Now we know that he was referring to the values of 'life worth living' (he uses that phrase later), those things which really make life worth living; but let us interpret this in the realm of heavenly things. The passage will bear repeated reading. He proceeds:

'The man must feel this, feel that indeed he has a worthy cause and that, if he did not defend it, life would not be worth the living. Nor was it enough to have a worthy cause—it must be positive, aggressive; not a mere passive, defensive and 'anti something' feeling, but positive and aggressive.'

All that is the foundation of morale. We need to lay it deeply to heart, for we are in something far bigger than the South East Asia Campaign. Far, far greater issues are at stake; a far greater Crown and Throne and Name and Government and Country are involved; a far greater enemy is in the field. And so Paul makes his appeal: "I therefore... beseech you...", and brings the whole matter of the battle for the Church's glorious consummation to this: "Finally, be strong in the Lord, and in the strength of His might. Put on the whole armor of God, that ye may be able to stand... Take up the whole armor of God, that ye may be able to withstand in the evil day".

"Be strong in the Lord"! May the Lord help us!

Intelligence and Diversity in Unity and Unity in Diversity

"That no advantage may be gained over us by Satan: for we are not ignorant of his devices" (2 Corinthians 2:11).

Intelligence

The next of the vital factors in our spiritual warfare that we are to consider is the matter of Intelligence. The above fragment of Scripture is quoted, not as a peg upon which to hang something, but as a key to very much more than its own context from which we may seem to be separating it. We refer again to the book from which many extracts have already been cited, the great record of the campaign that was conducted in South East Asia during the last war. Under the heading of 'Defeat'—to which subject, half of that long account is devoted, a sad and tragic part—there occur these words:

'Our Intelligence was extremely bad. We were like a blind boxer trying to strike an unseen opponent and to parry blows we did not know were coming until they hit us. The extreme inefficiency of our whole Intelligence system was probably our greatest single handicap.'

You will weigh all this, because it is most significant in the spiritual realm. The writer continues:

'The first thing to get right was the Intelligence organization. Until we could rely upon a reasonable degree of information we could not hope successfully to hold the enemy. We never made up for the absence of methodically collected Intelligence, which should have been available to us when the war began.'

Now these few extracts, if we carry them over into our warfare, are most enlightening, instructive and important.

Spiritual intelligence for spiritual warfare: that covers a very great deal of ground. As is so emphatically pointed out here, it is fundamental to the whole campaign. If we are lacking in spiritual intelligence, we shall be lacking in one of the vital requirements for victory. That is a well informed and considered judgment in the earthly realm; and, as we have repeatedly said, if it is true, as it has been proved to be, in the natural, how much more true it is in the spiritual—how much more is involved in this matter of intelligence in spiritual warfare!

Spiritual Intelligence Counters the Blinding Work of the Enemy

And so we pass from the natural warfare to the spiritual, the warfare in which you and I are, or should be, engaged.

We note, firstly, that God's whole scheme for our deliverance from Satan is based upon, or made effective by, spiritual intelligence, or spiritual enlightenment. We are told that, at the conversion of the Apostle Paul, in indicating his life work, his commission, the Lord said: "I send thee, to open their eyes, that they may turn from... the power of Satan unto God" (Acts 26:17–18). Here it is clearly assumed that, by nature, all men are in the power of Satan; and it is implied that they are there by reason of blindness. The nature of their bondage, of their captivity to Satan, and of his sway over them, that which gives it its power, its strength, is spiritual blindness. The way out, therefore, is not by means of an objective, external drive upon their captor, by trying to deal smashing blows at some imaginary spiritual force called 'Satan'. It is by means of an inward operation whereby spiritually blind eyes are opened, made to see. I repeat, therefore, that the whole scheme of man's deliverance from the enemy is based upon, and made effective by, spiritual enlightenment—that is, by spiritual intelligence.

(a) His Concealment of Himself and of Man's Condition

The enemy's supreme tactic in maintaining his power and his sway over mankind is along this line of keeping them in ignorance. One of his most successful devices is that of concealing himself—keeping man in ignorance of himself and of his work—and also of concealing from man his own condition. Man, of course, will not credit himself with blindness. It is a very difficult thing to make man believe that he is blind. Has he not intelligence, has he not common sense, has he not education, has he not many things, all of which he regards as enlightenment? The most difficult thing is to make him believe that he is blind; and that is a sure and certain proof that Satan has marvelously triumphed. He has hidden from man his own real condition, and has made him blind to his own blindness.

(b) His Interception of Knowledge

Another of the enemy's great tactics is to intercept all knowledge. There is a great deal in this book about reconnaissance, and the interception of reconnaissance: of how the enemy gained the upper hand, and secured his tremendous victory in the first campaign, very largely by completely crippling the reconnaissance arm of the opposing forces. The writer makes constant complaint and remonstrance about the absence or the failure of reconnaissance, and what it cost. In this matter of interception, of cutting off every agent and instrumentality that would bring intelligence to the opposing side, the enemy was in the unquestioned ascendant.

I do not propose to say much on the subject of our knowledge of the enemy, our information concerning him and his ways; I want to get on to something more profitable, more positive, than that. But this concern of the enemy to intercept intelligence, to cut it off, to make it impossible, to keep the Forces in ignorance, is an important factor, and we shall have to point it out as we go on.

The Apostle Paul, who, as we have already said, was a great fighter, a great warrior, was very much alive to this matter. He himself was up against this problem all the time. It would be a profitable line of study to collect all that Paul has written on the matter of enlightenment, of revelation, of intelligence, of spiritual understanding. For instance, it is impressive to realize that six times over, in different places and in different connections, Paul uses the phrase: "I would not have you ignorant..." (Rom. 1:13, 11:25; 1 Cor. 10:1, 12:1; 2 Cor. 1:8; 1 Thess. 4:13). If you take up the context of each of those six occasions, you will find that there is something of great significance bound up with each. "Brethren, I would not have you ignorant...", he says; and then follows something of vital importance.

Spiritual intelligence, then, is related in the first place to man's deliverance from the blinding and befogging activity of Satan.

The Inheritance Secured through Intelligence

In the second place, the whole basis of securing the inheritance of the people of God is that of spiritual intelligence. It is something more than being just saved. Salvation begins with spiritual enlightenment, the opening of the inward eyes. But thereafter, the pursuit of salvation to its ultimate objective, the fullness of Christ, is along the line of spiritual intelligence, illumination, understanding and knowledge. It matters not whether those words mean different things, or are inflections of the same thing; the issue is the same.

We know, for instance, that the Book of Joshua is the book of the inheritance. The people are going in to possess, to occupy, to exploit, to inherit. But what was the very first move, when Israel had come to the borders of the land, forty years previously? The setting up of Intelligence. Spies were sent to spy out the land. Joshua sent over intelligence officers, his Intelligence Corps. Intelligence was a tremendously important thing here. We might say that Joshua and Caleb were themselves the very embodiment of the principle of Intelligence. It was they who brought the report which, in the long run, resulted in a people going in and possessing. But note at this point an interesting and impressive and significant thing. The people thought to stone them! (Num. 14:10). You see, the enemy is not only over there in the land—he is entrenched in the very hearts of the people themselves, he has got a footing there. How true that is to principle and to history! Let any of the people of God begin to get some new light, and, as the Lord's instrument, they will become the object of Satan's hatred: he will stir up forces to stone that instrument. He hates instruments of spiritual enlightenment.

We pointed out, in chapter 2, that the Letter to the Ephesians is all of a piece: that, although there are progressive movements, it is nevertheless concerned with one thing—it concerns the Church coming into her inheritance. For the realization of that there is tremendous conflict. 'Principalities and powers and hosts of wicked spirits in the heavenlies' are arrayed against that, so it says. But what is it that precipitates the conflict, that makes it active, that brings us up against the evil forces? Paul is praying 'that the eyes of your heart may be enlightened, that you may know... that you may know... that you may know...' Therein is the explanation of the conflict. It all circles round this—'that the people of

God may know'. We do well to ask ourselves if we have really grasped that—if we are sufficiently alive to that.

Conclusions

(1) Progressive Intelligence Essential to Victory

What are the conclusions, then? Firstly, that intelligence, spiritual knowledge and understanding, are a very great factor for victory in this whole spiritual warfare. Do let us lay that to heart. We shall find it out and prove it sooner or later. The 'sooner' or 'later' depends upon whether we really grasp this fact. We shall not come through into full victory without spiritual understanding: we shall not get there willy nilly, just anyhow; we shall not drift into it; we shall not just find ourselves there. All along the way we shall find ourselves up against situations with which we shall be unable to cope, demanding a spiritual understanding and knowledge from the Lord without which we shall be unable to get through. The key to every further advance is more spiritual knowledge, more spiritual understanding. Without it, we shall be held up indefinitely.

Is that not true to experience? We come to an impasse, and have to go to the Lord; and, until the Lord gives light, we are locked up in that impasse. Once the light flashes; once we see; once we are able to say, 'Now I understand the meaning of this thing!'—the Devil's hold is broken, and we are released. If only we realized the background of situations, being quick on the scent to get the significance of happenings and not just taking them at their face value; if we were to say, 'Well, it all looks so natural, it all seems to have a very natural explanation of human fault and circumstance and what not, but there may be something else behind this'; if only we were more on the alert, it might be that we should not ourselves be knocked out of the fight, and other people who sadly needed our help would not be deprived of it. Satan lays his schemes very deeply, and covers them up so cunningly, does he not? He argues, 'Well, you see, it was this and that and some other thing.' Oh, no, it was not!—and even if it was, it should not have had this effect upon us.

Spiritual intelligence, then, is a tremendous factor in spiritual warfare and in spiritual growth and progress. 'That we may know... that we may know...'—and therein is a great battle!

(2) Intelligence Must Lead to Action

The second thing in our conclusions is that our intelligence, our knowledge, must be followed by action. It must be practical knowledge, not merely theory. We have all the theory of spiritual warfare in the Bible, have we not? We have the whole scheme from Genesis to Revelation! But are we applying it? Is it applied knowledge, or is it only theoretical? Is it followed by action? Or, when a situation arises, does all the theory we possess fail to serve any useful purpose? Does it fail to come to our rescue? Our knowledge must be applied, and practical knowledge. It must lead to action.

(3) The Need for Watchfulness Against Enemy Induced Inertia

Thirdly, the enemy's special concern is to keep God's people from increased spiritual knowledge, and that statement covers a great deal of ground. So often, when the Lord is purposing to impart to His children some particular spiritual knowledge, there comes over them a strange inertia: and that kind of inertia can sometimes be sinister. It is something more than mere tiredness or weariness; it seems to come over us suddenly, for no apparent reason. I have often, during a long experience, seen the children of God robbed of something vital through succumbing to that feeling of inertia and staying at home at such a time.

We need to weigh up our inclinations to stay at home, and judge them. There are times when it may be of the Lord that we remain quiet and alone at home, but let us be careful that we are not just being smothered by the enemy, in order that we may be robbed of something. Oh, the unwatchfulness of God's people! What loss it leads to! Yes, the Devil will create an inertia, or raise up some difficulty, some impediment, some circumstance, just to intercept—just to make sure that you are not there on some occasion; and then, like Thomas, when the Lord comes in you are absent. You know, that is a loss which is not easily recovered, and it may lead to some very real defeat in coming days. The very thing that you needed for a coming situation may have been there, provided by the Lord. Because you were not alive to the meaning of what was happening, and accepted the circumstance or the event at its face value, you missed some spiritual gain. How important this is! How very much alive we must be, 'intelligent unto intelligence'! As Paul says, "with all prayer and supplication praying... and watching thereunto..." (Eph. 6:18).

(4) The Enemy's Opposition to an Enlightening Ministry

Finally, opposition to a ministry which would make God's people spiritually strong is one of Satan's very definite activities. There is much history behind that statement. If there is a ministry—I am not thinking only of personal ministry—or any other instrumentality which can minister to a fuller knowledge of the Lord and to an understanding of His purposes concerning His Church, then not only the ministry itself, but the instrument of that ministry, the vehicle and the vessel of that ministry, and the place of that ministry, will all be an object against which Satan will be determinedly set— for its undoing, for its breaking down, for its disintegration, for its paralysis; somehow—anyhow—to destroy that instrument of ministry. Would that we might be fully alive to this!

Diversity in Unity and Unity in Diversity

What an immense variety of functions go to make up an efficient and effective fighting force! Almost endless are the auxiliaries and the complementaries, both of activities and of means. In an army, you have a large number of definite 'sub-forces', or contributing forces. Think of some of the main branches known to us: the Army Service Corps, for supplies; the Engineers, electrical and mechanical, for all installations and repairs and construction; the Ordnance Corps, for a large variety of things such as surveying, mapping, routeing, and so on; the Pay Corps, which is quite an important one, to see that men get their due and their rights (and it is strategic to do that: if there is a grumble in that realm you may upset the whole organization!); the Intelligence Corps, of which we have just spoken; and the Medical Corps, dealing with the whole matter of health and healing and care, and numerous other duties. Here are many, many functions; and yet, both within these main branches and without, there are almost countless details, committed to different people, all of which are essential.

And here is a really magnificent little paragraph from the book. What it says is good, but that it should be said by a Field Marshal is almost better, for it indicates that right at the top, notwithstanding all the great responsibilities and the important position and the name, the smallest detail was not overlooked. He has been speaking about the man right up in the battle front, who is aware of his responsibility, aware of the effect and influence of his behavior and his demeanor; and he goes on:

'But it is harder for the man working on the road, far behind, the clerk checking stores in a dump, the telephone operator monotonously plugging through his calls, the sweeper carrying out his menial tasks, the quartermaster's orderly issuing boot laces. I say it is harder for these and a thousand others to see that they, too, matter. You may be one of the half million in the Army, but you have to be made to see where your menial task fits into the whole scheme of things, and to realize what depends on it and on you, and, moreover, to feel pride and satisfaction in doing it.'

You see what I mean? Diversity in unity—unity in diversity. Many Scriptures will come to mind: *"There are diversities of gifts, but the same Spirit... all these worketh the one and the same Spirit" (1 Cor. 12:4,11).* Paul has a great deal to say about this matter of diversity in unity and unity in diversity. And the Lord would have it to be found in the Church.

The Holy Spirit: Sufficient, Indispensable, Sovereign

Now, let us seek to realize, first of all, that the Holy Spirit is comprehensive of all needs for this great campaign; that is, He covers the whole ground of what is required. He Himself is the supply and the dynamic, the ability for every section and every department and every function. He comprehends the whole and leaves out nothing that is essential. He covers everything. To put that another way, in the Holy Spirit there is everything that is required of ability, of faculty, of gift, of enablement, for this whole campaign, in all its departments and details. He is given to the Church to be all that.

But the next step is to realize that the Holy Spirit is given to each one, personally, with the object of making each one a functioning factor in the great campaign. There ought not to be a single individual in Christ who is not counting in this battle, who is not a vital factor in it, who is not really telling, who is not in some way making a contribution. If such 'non-functioning members' should exist, there is something wrong, because the manifestations of the Spirit are given to us "to profit withal", says the Word (1 Cor. 12:7). "Given to each for the profit of all", is Conybeare's rendering: that is, to make us a part of the inclusive profit and gain. And if we are not a vital factor in this warfare, it means that the Holy Spirit is somehow being hindered, checked, thwarted, frustrated in us. There is something wrong in our relationship to the Holy Spirit.

Thirdly, the Holy Spirit gives gifts as He will; that is, He is sovereign. It is not for you or for me to say what we are going to do in the Army, what place we are going to hold, what work we are going to do. That is the prerogative of the Holy Spirit. We have only to recall Paul's words, at the conclusion of the passage we have already quoted (1 Cor. 12:11), about the gifts of the Holy Spirit being distributed as He wills. You and I, therefore, should claim, as our very birthright, that the Holy Spirit should qualify us in some way to be a functioning member of this great Army—whether it be as 'the quartermaster's orderly distributing bootlaces', or whether it be something that we might think far more important: although it would certainly be a serious matter if a fighting soldier had not got his bootlaces!

What I mean, of course, is this. All these things are necessary; they are essential to the whole. It is not for us to say that ours is too little a job—that it does not matter. It does matter; yes, right down to a 'bootlace' it matters in this whole. And it is not just the nature of the job that you and I may be doing, or be given to do, that makes it important. It's importance lies in its relationship to the whole. Nor is it a question of personal importance—it is not that you or I are so important; any importance we may have comes from our relationship to the whole. And so we need to seek adjustment in this matter.

It is my firm belief that the Holy Spirit would in some way qualify, for quite definite functioning in this warfare, every member, every individual. For, in this 'unity in diversity', where everything is so related, every member is significant.

The Incentive of a Sense of Vocation and a Spirit of Service

I close with a word about the saving value of a sense of vocation, of service. If only we had this awareness of the greatness of the thing that we are in! If only we had a new sense that, as recipients of the Holy Spirit, we are those who should count, should signify: for that is why we have received the Holy Spirit—to make us count. And it matters about us. It does not matter to us about ourselves, but it does matter to the whole order of things. If only we had a due sense of that, what a great deal we should be saved! If our attitude is: 'I don't matter, I don't count', what is the result before long? A miserable life!

I recently read an article about self-pity, in which the story was told of how the help of a psychiatrist was sought by a woman who said that she had a nervous breakdown coming on. She evidently expected him to take a lot of trouble and analyze her history and give her some comforting words of advice. But he said: 'My dear woman, go home, turn the key in your front door, make your way to that poor district down there across the railway, find somebody who is in need of help, and get busy, and your nervous breakdown will never come off!'

There is much good, Divine common sense in that. We are enlarged by giving. We lose nothing by giving; our increase comes along the line of giving, of turning outward. Yes, "always abounding in the work of the Lord", always turned outward; animated by a spirit of service, seeking to be useful or helpful wherever we can; not just with a Bible under our arm, ready to go and speak at a meeting, but in all sorts of practical ways being a spiritual and physical help to the Lord's children. That is the way, not only of saving us from a miserable existence, but of bringing ourselves enlargement.

That is very practical and it is very true. The Spirit is given to us "to profit withal"! The Holy Spirit can enable us to be of value in ways that we cannot be naturally. Where would most of us be if we were left to ourselves, to our own natural resources, gifts and abilities—or lack of them? We should be of no use at all, for we have nothing. But the Spirit makes up wonderfully for our deficiencies; He really does make good our short-comings. By the Spirit's aid, every one of us can and should and must be counted in the battle.

Mentality, or Attitude of Mind

"For though we walk in the flesh, we do not war according to the flesh (for the weapons of our warfare are not of the flesh, but mighty before God to the casting down of strong-holds); casting down imaginations, and every high thing that is exalted against the knowledge of God, and bringing every thought into captivity to the obedience of Christ" (2 Corinthians 10:3–5).

Taking the latter part of the above passage: "Casting down imaginations" (the margin gives as an alternative "reasonings")... and bringing every thought into captivity to the obedience of Christ", we will now look together at the matter of mentality in relation to this great spiritual warfare. The perils and threats to victory of a wrong mentality; the tremendous advantage of a right mentality. I am again drawing upon the book to which reference has been made throughout these chapters. Although, in that book, the word 'mentality' is not specifically employed, what I am saying is certainly found there in substance.

A Wrong Mentality as to the Higher Command

Returning to the subject of our first consideration—that of the Supreme Command—let us state at once that there exist perils of a wrong mentality concerning the Lord Jesus, the Supreme Commander of all the Forces in the field which go by the name of the Church. The wrong mentality concerning Him is this: that He is One from whom to get everything, instead of the One to whom to give everything. There is a great danger of always thinking in terms of what we are to get from Headquarters, of what advantages are to accrue to us, of drawing toward ourselves: in effect—although we should never admit this—really putting ourselves, our interests, in the place of those of the Supreme Command; for that is how it works out.

It is just at this point that 'popular' Christianity has done a great deal of harm. Christianity has been put upon a wrong basis, or perhaps, to be a little more charitable, upon an inadequate basis, and the preaching is almost exclusively in terms of what we are to get. We are to get salvation; we are to get eternal life, peace, joy and satisfaction—all this and Heaven as well! But the emphasis is so largely upon what we are to get from the Lord Jesus, our Supreme Commander. It is at least an inadequate mentality, if not an altogether wrong one when it is a made a principle; it is a misinterpretation of the whole Christian life. We will come back to that in a moment. The right mentality—and, mark you, the only one that is going to serve the great purpose and to minister to the great objective—is the mentality that is governed by the principle: 'Give everything to the Lord'; not 'Get everything from the Lord.'

This is the governing principle of the Godhead, the principle that to give is the way of fulfillment. In the case of the Lord Jesus, that is made very clear in one classic passage of the Apostle Paul. We are told that He "emptied Himself... becoming obedient even unto death, yea, the death of the cross. Wherefore also God highly exalted Him, and gave unto

Him the name which is above every name" (Phil. 2:7–9). Fulfillment, the restoration of His voluntarily laid aside fullness, came to Him along the line of emptying, giving, pouring out. For that is, I repeat, the principle of the Godhead, and it is to be the mentality of all those who are engaged in this great warfare. We shall be knocked about, brought up short, arrested, defeated, just in so far as we are all the time thinking in terms of what should come to us. Let us make no mistake about it: it will be like that. The self-centered life is always the discontented life. The possessive life is the circumscribed life.

But the outgoing life is the life of abundant return—it all comes back. "Give, and it shall be given unto you; good measure, pressed down, shaken together, running over" (Luke 6:38). Those are the words of the Lord Jesus. Do you want eternal possessions? The way to receive—but don't do it with this motive—is to give. That is the principle. You see the wrongness of the kind of mentality about the Lord Jesus that feels He should all the time be giving, giving; that we must more and more receive from Him; that He is only there for our benefit! You see how false that is, how unsound and how dangerous; because, immediately we find that He is not giving like that and things are becoming a little difficult, we lose interest in the whole matter, and become paralyzed in battle, helpless as fighters, impotent in service. It is due to a wrong mentality about the Supreme Command. He is there to receive the honor and the glory and the riches, and the dominion and the power, and everything. And while He will give and give and give, eternally give, our relationship to Him must be on the basis, not of how much we are going to get, but of how much He is going to get from us.

A Wrong Mentality as to the Christian Life

Secondly, there are the perils of wrong ideas about the Christian life. There is the prevalent idea that the Christian life is merely a matter of being saved and being blessed; salvation and blessing, and all that goes with salvation. For many, this is the sum of the Christian life; this is how it is put by many Christian preachers and leaders, and this is the mentality which is encouraged. But the Word of God makes it perfectly clear that the Christian life is something far more than that. Our mentality, or 'mindedness', concerning it, should be that of being involved in, and a part of, the great conflict of the ultimate elemental forces of this universe.

For that is the issue. Long, long ago, something tremendous was set in motion; and ever since then, down through the centuries, the great purpose of God has been challenged and disputed. All through these generations the people of God, men of God, have given themselves in relation to that one great battle in the universe; and it still goes on—it is not at an end yet. The real nature of the Christian life is that you and I, immediately we become related to the Lord Jesus Christ, are called into that, involved in that. We are involved in what I have called the ultimate elemental forces of this universe in conflict: no less than the whole hosts of the Kingdom of God and of Heaven, on the one side, and, on the other side, this vast and vicious kingdom of Satan.

That is the Christian life! Do not have any illusions about it! The Lord Jesus allowed no one to have illusions about it: "Whosoever doth not bear his own cross, and come after Me, cannot be My disciple" (Luke 14:27). "Whosoever would save his life shall lose it; but whosoever shall lose his life for My sake, the same shall save it" (Luke 9:24). You see, that is straight, frank, candid and honest. This is what we are in! It is a great privilege to be in it, a great honor to be in it, but that is it. Let us have no wrong mentality about this. Through getting a wrong mentality about it, many people have become disappointed. They wonder, sometimes; they say: 'Well, I did not bargain for this; this is not what I expected, this is not what I became a Christian for. They told me that my life was going to be full of joy and happiness and peace, that everything was going to be beautiful and lovely, and that I would have a wonderful time—but now what have I landed into?' Well, there is joy and there is peace; there is all that, thank God; but we have to recognize and to adjust to the fact that we are in a battle, a fierce, unrelenting battle; and there is no discharge from the battle in this life.

A Wrong Mentality as to the Church

Thirdly, there can be wrong ideas about the Army itself — that is, the Church: the Church is the Army. It is possible to have a wrong mentality about this. The wrong mentality that is possible—and I would say this with emphasis—is that the Army, the Church, is the end and the object of everything. Now, we say much about the greatness of the Church, and we in no way exaggerate in so doing. We speak of it in superlative terms, as 'God's masterpiece', and so on. We are encouraged by the Word of God to think of it as something great and wonderful, even magnificent. Yes, the Church is a very wonderful conception in the mind of God from eternity; the Church has a very large place in the Divine counsels; it is to be presented at last to the Lord Jesus as a glorious Church. I will not recount all the great things that have been or could be said about it.

But, when all has been said that could be said, we have still to say: The Church is not the object, it is not the end; the Church is not the ultimate! The Church is, after all, no more than the instrument; it is but the vessel, it is but the agent. There is something beyond the Church—the Church only exists for something else. Perhaps its greatness in fact derives from the 'super-greatness' of the object which it is to serve. Let us, then, not make the Church the end, the 'everything'; let us not think that we have to live only and utterly and ultimately for the Church. We have to remember that, just as the Army does not exist for itself, does not go out in the campaign, into the field, for itself, but in the interests of the sovereign and his kingdom, so the Church exists and engages in warfare solely for the glory of the Throne, for the glory of the One on the Throne, for the glory of the Kingdom. That is the object of the Church's existence.

If we have faulty ideas here, we shall find that they constitute a weakness. If we put the Church in the place of Jesus Christ, we shall find ourselves in trouble with the Holy Spirit. That is not in any way to displace or to belittle the Church: but the Church exists for Christ. All our Church conceptions, all our relationships in that connection, indeed everything to do with that, should be governed by the fact that everything is for Christ—it is for Christ's sake. Why the Church, and why all that is said about the Church and related life? It is for Christ's sake! We must regard them as being, not ends in themselves, but for the satisfaction of Christ. We must have a clear mentality on this matter, and put Him in His rightful place.

A Wrong Mentality as to Ministries

We come next to the matter of functioning in the Army, or, to speak in spiritual terms, the ministries, the functions. Here again we can have wrong, defective, faulty ideas and mentality, and it may be that we need to make a little adjustment over this matter. What is the real meaning and value of ministries? Is ministry just a question of imparting knowledge and information? A great amount of that is, of course, done, in and by ministry. But is that what it is for— just teaching? No, the function of this ministry is something more than the imparting of knowledge and information. We are an Army in the field, and what is needed in a day of battle is not lectures—it is provision for the actual need in which we are found. If we come to the ministry provided in a condition of conscious need, we are in a way of getting real value. But if we are only coming for the sake of attending meetings and hearing addresses and receiving more and more knowledge and information, we shall never thereby be qualified for this battle.

Do you see the point? Here is this background of conflict. From time to time the Supreme Command visits the various positions, gathers the staff together and reviews the situation: he assembles all his men and talks to them. But the scene is a scene of battle. It is a time of war, not of peace; the conditions prevailing are war conditions; the scene and circumstances are those of actual war. Why does he gather the men around? To give them lectures on the theory of military life? Not a bit of it! He calls them together in order to give help and instruction on how to meet the existing and immediate situation; to direct as to how to cope with that which confronts them, with that which they are up against right there and then.

And that ought to be the nature of all our meetings and our ministry. We ought all the time to be a people on a war footing, right up against emergencies, threats, perils and dangers. If we had that mentality, that we really are so engaged; that we are right up against a very persistent and cunning enemy; that we are in truth in the thick of the battle—our meetings would serve much greater purposes, our ministry would be of far greater value. Suffer this emphasis and stress. Our meetings must at all costs be redeemed from being just sessions of theory. We can reach saturation point in that way, so that we are unable to take any more. But if we are right in this battle, and really meaning business, if we are up against things and want help, we shall go where help is to be found. We ought to be at our meetings on this footing: 'I need it, I cannot do without it, my situation demands it.' But if there is no demand, how valueless will be the supply! We need to get our mentality adjusted over this. Our meetings and ministry must represent a provision for immediate, actual need.

And if we really are in the business, the Lord will see to it that we are in need, all right! He will make things very practical, very real. He will see to it that our Christian lives are constantly brought up against new needs. Do not worry, do not think things have gone wrong, if you find yourself up against a situation for which you have no answer! The Lord is doing that to keep you moving on. Our progress is only along that line, on the basis of growing need. Immediately that stops, we stop. We go no further than our sense of need—and our very acute sense of need. The Lord keeps most of us there, does He not?—in a way of very real, practical need: more need, and ever more need. Blessed be God! He only does it in order that the need may be supplied. But when things become a matter of course, a matter of habit, a matter of—'Well, we are going along to the meeting because it is meeting night'—then we simply make every supply dead. May the Lord bring us together every time as in uniform, that is, on a war footing, as in a council of war.

All ministry must have a practical background, both for giving and for receiving. God save those of us who minister from ministering just theories and material! The Lord keep all who minister on the basis of a very practical background, so that what is ministered is born out of experience and actuality in life. The ministry must not consist in searching out matter and putting it together and retailing it as addresses. Not at all! It must be born out of life, right up to date. And there must be active exercise on both sides—in those who minister and in those who receive. It must be a practical matter: there must be action about it. There must be, on the part of all, a very serious quest, the seriousness of which is born of the desperateness of the situation: the situation being that, unless we have this knowledge from the Lord, unless we have life from the Lord, we are going under in the battle, the enemy is going to gain. That is the nature of those councils of war, those 'conferences', those meetings with our Supreme Commander, to which we sometimes gather. They are just that we may be equipped for our job—and our job is fighting. Our object at all such meetings should be to get equipment for our very life work, which is now on hand.

A Wrong Mentality as to Others

Lastly, we come to wrong ideas concerning the other personnel in the Army—the other people in the Church. We have many wrong ideas about one another. Some of them are hardly worthy of mention. You know how easy it is to be selective, to look at the other man or woman and write them off as not counting for much, saying, 'Now this one, you know, this one counts for something, means something; this one has got measure. But that other one, well—no.' Be very careful! That is dangerous. Our kind of selectiveness, our judgment of people, may sabotage the whole movement. And, after all, what about ourselves? Where would you be, where would I be, if the Lord had been very particular, very particular indeed, to have the right measure and stature and quality? Where would I be? where would you be? I know where I would be: I would not be in this warfare or ministry! I settled it with the Lord, long ago, that He must provide all the qualifications to keep me in. But, you see, He has to do that with the others as well, and He can. We must be very careful about this matter.

We must be very careful, too, that we do not, as is sometimes done, contemplate others as competitors and rivals who are seeking to get an advantage over us. We must not be 'touchy' about our own position and our own rights and prerogatives; we must not be very touchy and explosive if someone else is put before us, or seems to have been put in our place, given a favor, and so on. It is a horrible thing to think of such an attitude amongst Christians, but it can happen only too easily. By taking personal offence, because of something that has been done that seems to be placing us at a disadvantage, we can be put out of the fight at once—put right out of the battle! In such a situation, whether we judge it to be right or wrong, our attitude must be this: 'Lord, I am Yours, I am Your man, I am in this for You. Men can do what they like—put me out, put others over my head; they can do what they like. That is between You and me, Lord, and between You and them.' You see, if you allow yourself to take offence, be hurt and grieved because of others, the enemy can come in on that ground, and you will become a casualty—you may as well be carried out on a stretcher straight away! If you are going down in that way you are no use to the fight. Be careful! Let us be careful of our attitudes, of our mentality, when it involves other people.

That could be enlarged upon, but we leave it there, with just the reminder that a favorite maneuver of our enemy is to get amongst us and make us look at one another and misjudge one another, misinterpret one another, and mistrusting one another. And what is the good of an Army like that—all looking at one another with questions or suspicions or hurt feelings! What a state of mind! The word is: "Casting down imaginations"—and, if we only knew all the truth, we should discover that a great deal of it is imagination; it is not real. We should find that, after all, that was not meant, that was not the implication at all; it was our imagination—it was how it came to us and our imagination got busy on it. And we are put out! Clever maneuver of the enemy! The counter to that is found in our passage: "our warfare... casting down imaginations... and bringing every thought into captivity to... Christ". Do it now! Lay hold of those thoughts that have done you injury and perhaps done someone else injury. Lay hold of them! They will make you unfit for battle; they will affect the whole issue; they will touch others in the Army. There is a great deal of Scripture behind that, if we like to call it up. Lay hold of those thoughts and bring them into captivity to Christ. Make sure that you are right, and, even if you are right, be prepared to forgive, to be charitable, and at any rate not to make a personal issue of it.

A Wrong Mentality as to Ourselves

How prone we are to have wrong ideas about ourselves! Paul said: "I say... to every man that is among you, not to think of himself more highly than he ought to think" (Rom. 12:3a). What ought you to think of yourself, what ought I to think of myself? In the light of God's grace, of God's mercy, of God's love, in the light of God's holiness, what ought we to think of ourselves? "...Not to think of himself more highly than he ought to think; but", continues Paul, "so to think as to think soberly, according as God hath dealt to each man a measure of faith" (vs. 3b); that is, if we may take another word of Paul's out of its context, "according to the measure of the gift of Christ" (Eph. 4:7). The measure of our self-esteem will be in inverse proportion to the measure of Christ that we have. How much of Christ have we received? Well, if we have a superabundance of Christ, if we have more of Christ than anyone else, we shall not think highly of ourselves at all. The more we have of Christ, the less we shall think of ourselves, the less we shall want to talk about ourselves, the less we shall be in view, the less we shall want to be in the limelight.

"Every man... not to think of himself more highly...". What ravages such a wrong mentality could make in an Army! Just imagine what would happen if men behaved like that —thinking more highly of themselves than they ought to think, 'throwing their weight about', as we say. No, that will not do; that is only playing into the hands of the enemy. Our safety lies in 'thinking soberly', according as each of us has received of the measure of Christ. In this great battle, it matters greatly what kind of mind we have. "Have this mind in you, which was also in Christ Jesus..." In an earlier chapter we have urged that everyone should realize that, in a related way, the army depends upon the units: that the whole can suffer through the weakness of the individual. Thus it works both ways. We can overestimate our personal importance, or we can underestimate our related significance. To think of ourselves as we ought to think will mean that we do not err in either direction: we shall recognize that it does matter about us, but that it matters relatively, and not just personally—that is, independently.

Discipline, Provisioning and Flexibility

> *"Suffer hardship with me, as a good soldier of Christ Jesus. No soldier on service entangleth himself in the affairs of this life; that he may please him who enrolled him as a soldier"*
> *(2 Timothy 2:3,4)*

(A) Discipline

In these well-known words of Paul, we are introduced to the most important matter of discipline. What is discipline? It could be described as the steadying effect, the girding power, of purposefulness, as opposed to looseness and carelessness and slackness. It is what the Apostle Peter calls "girding up the loins of your mind" (1 Pet. 1:13). Now, in that great South East Asia Campaign to which we have been referring, discipline had, naturally, a very large place. We will consider it in its connection with five different, though related, things.

(1) As to Behavior

In the first place, discipline is related to behavior. I am not quoting from the volume, but there is a great deal said about this matter of behavior. It is so easy to accept the subtle idea that, when you are on a war footing (especially under conditions such as obtained in that campaign), discipline does not matter so much: you can throw off the restraints of the parade ground and need not bother about the strict rules and regulations of training; you are free from all that and can just plunge straight into the battle. But the writer of this book makes much of the importance of bringing into the battle all those rules of training and discipline and behavior. And you will at once see that our behavior as the Lord's people is a most vital factor in the campaign. The New Testament, as we know, has a great deal to say about Christian behavior, and it is not without very real purpose that the Lord makes such large mention of it in His inspired volume. He knows the importance of our conduct, our demeanor—of how we behave. With Him it is a vital part of the battle. It matters; it makes a great deal of difference. We are not to be slack, loose, careless, in our way and manner of life. The enemy makes great gain out of that sort of thing; it puts a most effective weapon into his hand against the Lord's interests, against the whole object to which we are called.

You and I, as Christians, have got to watch our behavior: not only before the world, but—as we shall emphasize again presently—even in secret. It matters whether we are disciplined in the matter of behavior. The great point that this book makes of behavior is that discipline should have become second nature: it should not merely be something put on for the occasion, when it is expected and when eyes are on us, when we are more or less on parade before the officers. We should not need to be told or pulled up. Disciplined behavior should become second nature; it should just be us—we are that. Our behavior should betoken what we are.

A simple point is made by the Supreme Command in that connection. Soldiers, when they are on the parade ground or in training, are, of course, very careful about the saluting of officers; it is a part of their discipline. But it was noticed that, when they were all mixed up in battle conditions, officers and men together under actual war conditions, they became very slack, very careless and loose, in this seemingly small matter. And the Supreme Command said: This is something that shows whether men are really trained men or not; it gives them away. If they were really disciplined men, the conditions under which they live would make no difference at all: they would carry out the rules and regulations of their training under all circumstances, for it would have become second nature. They would salute an officer just as much in those active service conditions, even in jungle warfare, as they would on the parade ground or in training.

This illustration should impress upon us the importance of realizing that discipline is not just something artificial, something that we assume; it is not just the behavior that we put on when we are being watched and when it is expected of us. It is how we behave when we are caught off-guard that reveals what we are. While that may sound very simple and elementary, it is a very important thing in the Christian life. The discipline of the Holy Spirit in our lives will show itself under all conditions: we act so, because we are that—that is what we are. When we are in public, where we know that it matters what people think of us, we can put on mannerisms, assume an artificial voice, pose, effect. But when we are with a few, for whom we have not a great deal of respect, we can put off the guise and really show our true nature. This is fatal to reality!

(2) As to Care for Health

Then there was the matter of discipline in regard to health. It was of the utmost importance that every care and precaution related to health should be most carefully, most meticulously observed. But terrible havoc was wrought in that campaign by disease; many thousands of men were lost to the fighting forces through carelessness in the matter of health.

How much more urgent, then, is care of health in the spiritual realm! It is very important that you and I should be disciplined in the matter of spiritual health. In Latin, the word for 'health' is cognate with our word 'salvation'; and salvation connotes 'preservation', 'deliverance'. Discipline in spiritual health means to be alive to the perils to spiritual life, the threatening inroads to the spiritual condition. Very much could be said on the matter of spiritual maladies, spiritual diseases, spiritual infirmities. Many of them overcome us because we are not disciplined, we are not careful, we are not watchful; we are not alive to things that can undermine our spiritual health. It is of great importance for the battle that we should be spiritually healthy, be in good health and strength. This is something of which to take real account. The question on any given issue should be—not: Is it right or wrong? (in a permissive sense)—but: Will this unfit me for the battle? will this in any way weaken me in the great campaign in which I am engaged?

You see, it is fitness for the fight that matters, but the peril of carelessness over it is ever present. So, to the man to whom the Apostle says: "Suffer hardship as a good soldier of Jesus Christ", he will also say: "Lay hold on eternal life" (1 Tim. 6:12, A.V.). There are times when we are slack in this matter: we need life, and there is life available, but we do not lay hold of it as we should—we just let go. A disciplined Christian is one who will say in the time of threatening or actual weakness: 'This is the time for me to lay hold on life, not to give way, not to let go. If I let go, I shall be put out of the fight. I must put up my defenses against these things that would weaken; I must react to this situation; I must resist; I must lay hold on life.'

I can but hint at what I mean, but if you had read the terrible account of the decimation of the forces in this campaign by disease, through carelessness as to health, you would see that there is point in this. And we have an enemy who, in a spiritual sense, is constantly sending germs our way, with the object of putting us out; but there is such a thing as really laying hold on life, being strong to resist, and maintaining our spiritual strength by the grace of God.

(3) As to Selflessness

A further aspect of discipline relates to the need of being always alive to the fact that what we do or fail to do involves others. An illustration is given in this book of how that worked out in the case of one particular man (and maybe of others through his example), who was on sentry duty under war conditions. He was extremely, desperately tired, almost exhausted, and yet he had a very important point to guard. Many lives were involved in the matter of his alertness. So, having to stand on guard in one place, quietly and alone, for long hours of the night, what did he do? He put his rifle in front of him with the bayonet fixed, and he put his chin on the point of the bayonet, so that if he nodded—well, he knew what would happen. Because of others! That was something the Commander in chief took note of, that the man should do a thing like that because of his sense of responsibility. To have nodded, to have gone off to sleep at that moment, would maybe have given the enemy the advantage. We know what the New Testament says about Satan getting an advantage (2 Cor. 2:11).

But here again, the point of discipline is the realization that we do not live to ourselves or die to ourselves (Rom. 14:7); that in what we do we involve others. That has already been said in an earlier chapter; but let us hear the added emphasis as it comes up again in this connection. 'Now then, I must—or I must not—and not only because of myself. If it were only myself, well, what matter?' If it just began and ended with ourselves, we would sometimes perhaps let our lives go and our testimony go. But there is very much more in it. 'I dare not, I must not—or I must—because...'—because of others and because of the battle. Discipline calls for selflessness.

(4) As to Losing Heart

How great is the constant temptation, under the long-drawn out wear and tear of the campaign, to weaken, to lose heart, just to drop out, or to cease to be a positive factor. How often we have to pull ourselves up, do we not, under discouraging conditions, when we are inclined to feel it is not worth it, when inertia comes over us and we fall into a state of despondency and depression. That is the time when discipline is tested. The undisciplined just give way; the disciplined do not. Our reaction to the temptation to give up will be according to whether we have or have not been thoroughly disciplined. We are tested then; we are found out.

(5) As to Service

Finally, discipline is related to service. That was involved in what we said just now, but it is particularly so in regard to the spirit of service. In the book that we have been considering, it is clearly stated that there should be a spirit of service. I think that spirit is leaving the world, is being very largely lost to the world to day. There are very few left who have a spirit of service—shall I say, of servanthood. But the Lord Jesus said: "I am in the midst of you as he that serveth"

(Luke 22:27). "The Son of man came not to be ministered unto, but to minister" (Mark 10:45). It is not difficult to see the connection between service and discipline. Evidence of it is, indeed, provided by the association of the contrary conditions to these in the world today. The opposites go together: the loss of the spirit of service goes hand in hand with the loss of discipline.

The Lord's Concern for Discipline

Let us now bring this matter right over to our own lives as the Lord's people. It is very important for us to realize that the Lord Himself is most particular on this question of discipline. Perhaps we know it, in a way; perhaps we have come up against it; and yet maybe we have not given it much thought—we have not looked it straight in the eyes and recognized it. The Lord Himself is very particular about discipline. Whether we do or not, the Lord views everything from the standpoint of the war. He has filled the Bible with this matter of warfare. He Himself is declared to be "a man of war" (Ex. 15:3). The Lord knows that there is a war on, and He knows everything about it. We may think we know a little about it, but He has complete cognizance of the full extent and range of this spiritual war that is in progress. For it is a terrific conflict that is raging between these two great kingdoms and powers and systems. And so He views everything from the standpoint of the war, and deals with us on the basis of war conditions. He is therefore most particular about this matter of discipline.

Now, let your imagination rove over such a point of view, and at once you will see why the Lord is very strict with us. He would say to us, in effect: 'Do you not realize that you are in a great conflict? Do you not realize that you are—or at any rate are supposed to be—a soldier on active service, under war conditions, and subject to all the rigors of such conditions? In the light of this, what kind of Christian are you?' The Lord does not let us off; He pulls us up, He really keeps us on a basis of discipline, because He views everything from the standpoint of the war and its issue, whether we are effectives or not. Perhaps that is why He was seemingly a little unkind to Elijah under the juniper tree. 'What are you doing here? You are supposed to be in the battle! What are you doing here? The battle is on! We have just had one tremendous set to on the mount, but we are not through with this yet. What are you doing here?' But whether that be the right interpretation of the story or not, I find that very often the Lord challenges me like that: 'What are you doing here, what do you mean by this? What are you down there for? Are you forgetting that there is a war on and that you are in it?' So the Lord is careful, particular; He deals with us from that standpoint and on that basis.

And, as we said earlier, do not forget that the Lord takes account of us in secret. The parade ground is one thing, when everybody is looking on and we know what is expected of us before all eyes. But the Lord takes account of us in secret. He did of David. David was God's choice because He had watched him in secret—in secret responsibility. You and I must remember that God chooses and uses, promotes and advances, those who remain true without the incentive of publicity. Have you grasped that? Do you want the Lord to choose you, to use you, to advance you, to give you more responsibility, to promote you? He will do it, not by what you are in the public eye, but by what you are in secret: for it is there that discipline counts most—when there is nothing whatever to give us an incentive, other than, 'Well, there is a battle on, and we must count in it!'

Discipline, Provisioning and Flexibility

This covers, of course, a lot of ground. It explains so much of the Lord's dealings with us, does it not? That is why we have such discipline, why we are put into positions where it is so hard, where there is seemingly no inspiration, no encouragement, no incentive at all. We are brought into situations where we are either going to stand or fall, and sometimes the testing is the more intense because it seems to us not to matter which we do. That is a real test of discipline!

(B) Provisioning

We come now to a factor that will sooner or later vitally affect an Army and all the units which make up the Army — the matter of provisioning. There may be much enthusiasm at the setting out, a good deal of abandonment. There may be a great deal of initial good spirit and good intention. But the things that count in the long run are constitution and stamina and endurance, and those things depend upon provisioning, on supplies, on food. You know Napoleon's statement, do you not, about that on which an Army advances? He often quoted, 'An army marches on its stomach'. It is very true! And if it is true in the natural, it is equally, if not more, true in the spiritual. It is a very great mistake, indeed it positively imperils the Forces, to send them into the field on a hand to mouth basis of supply, without adequate support in resources. And in the story of which we are thinking, thinning ranks, disaffection, disintegration, and many other troubles arose because the men were not being properly fed, because adequate provisions were not available.

Provisioning a Vital Factor in Endurance

Food, then, is a vital factor in the whole strategy of war. Provisioning is, indeed, not a luxury—it is an absolute necessity; and that is true spiritually. You and I must put from our minds any idea that the obtaining of spiritual food is something optional, governed by whether we feel inclined for it or not. To have adequate resources available, and to make good use of them, is an essential part of the whole campaign. And so our attitude toward this matter has to be quite a serious one. The war depends upon our spiritual constitution, our powers of endurance, our stamina, and these in turn depend upon our feeding, upon the provision made. Fighting forces cannot continue indefinitely on stimulants, certainly not on 'dopes'; they need feeding.

But in the Christian world there is a lot of 'stimulating' and 'doping' going on that is not feeding. It is an endeavor to work something up, to get people going for a while; but it will not work when they come into situations where real endurance is called for. And so the Supreme Command takes account of this—it makes provision for a long term conflict; and the sooner we get adjusted to that, the better. There are those who may fight pretty well if they think it is all going to be over soon. But we know quite well, do we not, from history that it is those who can hold out the longest who win the day. How much there is in the New Testament about this whole matter of spiritual stamina, and endurance, and steadfastness! *"He that endureth to the end, the same shall be saved" (Matt. 10:22; 24:13).* (Compare Heb. 3:6,14; 6:11; Rev. 2:26).

Now, there is far more in this matter of the Lord providing spiritual food for us than perhaps we realize. Let us make no mistake about it: sooner or later we shall be found out over this. It will be those who have been nourished in spiritual things, built up in spiritual things; who have made good use of all the possibilities of spiritual food available: it will be they who will stand when the real test comes. Is it not true to our experience, even in quite a simple way, that very often when we are up against things we are able to draw upon what the Lord has taught us in the past? Without that reserve, we should be at a loss—we could not get through; but now we are all the time able to draw upon what the Lord has given us. How wonderfully it rises up, again and again, just as He promised (John 14:26), to save us in a critical hour and situation! We remember His word and His way in the past: and it counts, it amounts to something. But on the other hand, how many there are who just go out under the pressure, because they have no background—they have not that knowledge of the Lord which the occasion demands.

The Need for Concern Regarding God's Provision

But we need to remember that, while the Lord is only too willing and ready to make provision, He does demand that there be a concern for it on the part of those for whom the provision is to be made. I think that this goes to the heart of a great deal. There is, as you know, a widespread complaint about this matter of spiritual food: a complaint that there is so little available, so little real teaching, so little strong meat. However it may be put, there is quite a complaint about this food shortage. But may not the existence of the condition complained of be very largely due to an insufficient concern for spiritual food on the part of either the officers or the people? They have not been careful over the matter, not really concerned about it. They have been content to live upon a light diet of Christian things. The Lord will make resources available for those who really mean business. For those who are really right in the battle, who are really concerned about His honor and about the victory, the Lord will see that adequate supplies are there. If you and I are not of that mind and disposition, the Lord Himself will not 'cast His pearls before swine'—He will not give His spiritual riches to those who are not greatly concerned. But, if we are, then He will make the provision.

You see, the Lord always aims to make His provision profitable, by giving it over against a practical background. There has to be a practical background before we can profit by the provision the Lord makes. That is why He is constantly precipitating us into situations that make it necessary for us to know Him in some deeper way. Is it not a very familiar fact that what we have in the whole of the New Testament is given to us over against a very practical background? Men did not sit down to write essays and treatises, and that sort of thing. They were facing extremely critical situations, and they wrote to meet those situations. It was matters of life or death that drew out all these writings. That was the background; and what was true then is still true in our lives, that we shall never profit by the Lord's provision unless we have a practical background.

The Divine Provision—"The Bread of Life"

What we need to grasp is that the principle of food is life. It is not a matter of whether we like or dislike, whether we fancy or do not fancy, or whether we are 'finicky. It is not that at all. It is simply and entirely a matter of life—LIFE! That is why the Lord Jesus said; "I am the bread of life" (John 6:35). And if we are to profit by that Bread, there must be the same life in us as is in the Bread. There must be a correspondence of life—life taking hold of life and life ministering to life. It has to be a vital matter, not just interest.

It is a solemn fact that you can have a thorough going acquaintance with the Bible as a book, and you can attend all the Bible lectures that are going, and still not grow spiritually. I know that to be true. For some years I was closely associated with Dr. Campbell Morgan, as one of the members of his Bible Teachers' Association, the whole method of which was the analytical teaching of the Bible. But with all that, and years of it, many of the people who attended the Bible lectures showed little or no spiritual growth. Very few of them came to anything like spiritual maturity; they were still babes after they had heard it all. They had it all stored in their notebooks—they knew it in that way; but as for being vital factors in the great campaign, they counted for little or nothing.

No, it is not merely a question of knowing the Bible in that way, although that may be a useful thing as a foundation. The essential thing is that it should be a matter of life— indeed of life or death. Those are the two alternatives. Our very survival depends upon this matter of food.

And the food is Christ. The Lord Jesus did not say, 'I give you a volume of teaching to feed upon.' He said: "I am the bread of life"—'I, personally, am the bread of life'. And so before we can profit by the bread we must know a vital, practical relationship with Him. There has to be a life-relationship between the feeder and the food.

It is really a question of the kind of food. Different species require different kinds of food: the food of one class of creation differs from that of another. You and I could not live on the food of certain species of animal; they probably could not live on our kind of food. A spiritual person (which is to say a normal Christian) belongs to a species whose need can only be met by spiritual feeding: that is, by a real, living knowledge of the Lord; and it is that alone that will make for triumphant warfare. A 'natural', intellectual acquisition of knowledge of the Bible is no substitute for spiritual food.

Let us, then, seek to draw the important lessons from all this. Let us not think of spiritual provision as something that we can take or leave. Such an attitude will find us out in the battle, sooner or later. I believe that there are many in this world who are now discovering the tremendous value of all that they have been taught and have learnt of the Lord in the past, while others are finding that they have not the resource for going through.

(C) Flexibility

I quote again from the book: 'The hardest test of generalship is to hold the balance between determination and flexibility. In this the enemy failed. He scored highly by determination; he paid heavily for lack of flexibility.'

In case this word 'flexibility' should occasion difficulty, let us suggest some alternatives. For instance: adjustableness; adaptability; teachableness, or 'teachability'; resourcefulness; originality. These are all sidelights on the word 'flexibility'. In the South East Asia campaign, the quotation that I have given meant just this: that the enemy had got so much into a rut; he was so decided on a certain course, and was so rigidly bound by it, that if anything upset it he was completely demoralized. He had no alternative; he had no resourcefulness with which to meet a surprise, to meet something that was outside of his program. If things went off his set course, he was just thrown into confusion. As this quotation says, 'he paid heavily for his lack of flexibility'. Here we really have something to learn.

Perhaps we cannot make too much of the quality of determination. The New Testament is so full of the matter of steadfast endurance: being set on going on: not being turned aside; and this is right—we should be people like that. But you see what is said here: 'The hardest test of generalship is to hold the balance between determination and flexibility.'

When you get down to it, you find that that really is a hard lesson: it is a hard thing to learn how to adjust yourself to new situations, and yet remain steadfast. Happily, we have some illustrations of this in the New Testament, and we do not go very far into the history of the Church before we come on them.

(1) Peter and Cornelius

Now Peter had got his fixed way, his fixed position, according to the Old Testament and his interpretation of it. And from his fixed position, his rigid, static position, he would argue with the Lord: "Not so, Lord"! Until he had "thought on the vision" (Acts 10:19), and got through with the Lord on the matter, he was not flexible, he was not adjustable, he was not even teachable. But what a tremendous advance, not only for Peter, but for the whole Church, when, without giving away any steadfastness or determination, he adjusted to the new light that the Lord gave, to a new knowing of the Lord, and the way of the Lord. And yet many people cannot do that; they just cannot do it.

(2) Philip and the Ethiopian Eunuch

Take the incident of Philip and the eunuch. It is just the same principle. Philip was down at Samaria, and under the blessing of the Lord wonderful things were happening. Philip could easily have said, 'The Lord is blessing me, the Lord is doing a great thing: I ought therefore not to leave this—this is where the Lord is working, this is what the Lord is doing', and so on. Well, of course it depends upon whether the Lord tells you to or not. But it also depends on whether you are open to the Lord: upon your having no fixity or finality about your position, but being ready to be moved by the Lord— even though it may seem a strange kind of move to be transferred from a revival center, with many coming to the Lord, to an almost empty desert.

Nevertheless, it meant no small advance for the Church that Philip was flexible. For the matter did not end with a desert. From that point there opened up for Philip a long story of ministry. We are not now dealing with New Testament development or history; but you will find, if you look into it, that, after this contact with the Ethiopian, some very vital things came into being through the ministry of Philip. And it all hung upon this matter of flexibility, adjustableness; on whether the Lord was free to have His way in that life, or whether Philip would say, 'No: this is where I am and this is how things are; this is what the Lord is doing and where He is doing it; and here I stay'! It may be that comparable issues are in the balance in the lives of many servants of the Lord to day.

(3) *Paul and Macedonia*

One more illustration—and it is a very great one, is it not?—Paul and Macedonia. Paul was set on going to Asia and Bithynia. But he came to the point where he was brought up short—"forbidden of the Holy Spirit": "the Spirit of Jesus suffered them not" (Acts 16:6–7). But Paul was adjustable, that is the point; he was flexible. And so—Macedonia and Europe! and how much more!!

These three examples illustrate the principle of being open to the Lord, of being in the Lord's hands and not in your own, of not being under any fixed mind as to what the Lord should do, and where He should do it, or how He should do it—that is with Him. It is one of the most important principles that the Lord would teach us.

God's Unchanging Truths and Changing Methods

We have to recognize that there are two sets of things. On the one side there is fundamental truth, about which we are never flexible and from which we never depart. There can be no question of giving up fundamental truth, or of changing our foundations. On that we are—or should be—inflexible. We ought to be immovable, too, on the matter of the all governing object of God; as to that, we are set, and nothing will move us. And it is also required that we be found with steadfastness of spirit.

But, on the other side, we have to recognize that God changes His methods. While He does not change His truths and His foundations and His object, He changes His methods. He has in His own sovereign right the prerogative to do as He will, and to do a new thing that was never heard of before. But that is something that Christianity today, for the greater part, just will not allow! It will not even allow God Almighty to do something that He has never done before! The lines are set, the whole compass of truth is boxed; the methods are so and so, the recognized ways and means are these. Depart from these, and—well, you are unsafe, you are dangerous. There is no room allowed for the Holy Spirit to do new things. But herein is the balance: with the unchanging foundations of truth, unchanging object of God, unchanging steadfastness of spirit, on the one side, there is yet, with all that, a balance to be kept, on the other side, with God's changing methods, God's sovereign right to 'go off the lines' if He wills: for the lines may not be His lines at all—they may be man's lines. God says, "I will do a new thing", and His absolute right to do a new thing must be recognized.

So much, then, for flexibility. It is a very important thing. Fixity in tradition, immovability in certain doctrinal positions, is resulting in great misunderstanding and confusion, arrest and disintegration. Through this limiting of the Holy Spirit, much is being lost.

Now, even if we do not grasp or appreciate much of the details, there are simple lessons lying on the surface of these three things that we have considered.

1. Discipline. The Lord must have a disciplined people, and He is very particular about our discipline in all its connections—behavior, spiritual health, and so on.

2. Provisioning. The Lord would have a well-nourished people, and He would have us careful about our spiritual food, to guard it. The enemy has a real eye to

business on the food of God's people, as Gideon will tell us (Judges 6:3–4, 11).

3. Flexibility. The Lord's desire is that, while we should be very steadfast and immovable as to those things which are fundamental to the faith, and in spirit, and in relation to His ultimate end, we should yet be so open to Him, so teachable, as to be, in a right way, pliable; in a right way, yes, changeable. There is much paradox about all these things, is there not? It is wrong to be changeable in some ways, but when it is the Lord calling for this adjustableness to Himself and what He would do, it is certainly right, and our response may, indeed, affect the whole issue of the war.

These things, presented to us in the Word by illustration and incident, embody very important principles. But when all is said, it comes back to this—everything strengthens this matter: We are in a war—a war that is no mere vague, abstract, 'airy fairy' kind of thing, but is very real, with many practical matters relating to the issue. These practical matters of behavior, of provisioning, and of adjustability, all relate to the issue of this war.

The Lord teach us, then, the laws of—

OUR WARFARE!

Made in the USA
San Bernardino, CA
04 January 2016